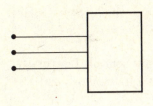

D0303464

# PRIVATIZATION AND
# REGULATORY CHANGE
# IN EUROPE

ONE WEEK
LOAN

MAR 1998

7
7

)97

1 7 MAR 1998

# LAW AND POLITICAL CHANGE

*Series Editors*: Professor Cosmo Graham, Law School, University of Hull, and Professor Norman Lewis, Centre for Socio-Legal Studies, University of Sheffield.

Current titles:

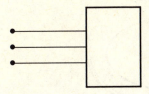

# PRIVATIZATION AND REGULATORY CHANGE IN EUROPE

EDITED BY

Michael Moran and Tony Prosser

OPEN UNIVERSITY PRESS
Buckingham • Philadelphia

Open University Press
Celtic Court
22 Ballmoor
Buckingham
MK18 1XW

and
1900 Frost Road, Suite 101
Bristol, PA 19007, USA

First Published 1994

WL
338.94
MO

Copyright © The editors and contributors 1994

All rights reserved. Except for the quotation of short passages for the
purposes of criticism and review, no part of this publication may be
reproduced, stored in a retrieval system, or transmitted, in any form or
by any means, electronic, mechanical, photocopying, recording or
otherwise, without the prior written permission of the publisher or a
licence from the Copyright Licensing Agency Limited. Details of such licences
(for reprographic reproduction) may be obtained from the Copyright
Licensing Agency Ltd of 90 Tottenham Court Road, London, W1P 9HE.

A catalogue record of this book is available from the British Library

ISBN 0 335 19072 3 (pbk)   0 335 19073 1 (hbk)

*Library of Congress Cataloging-in-Publication Data*
Privatization and regulatory change in Europe / Michael Moran and Tony
  Prosser (editors).
      p.    cm. — (Law and political change)
  Includes bibliographical references and index.
  ISBN 0–335–19073–1    ISBN 0–335–19072–3 (pbk.)
  1. Privatization — Europe. 2. Deregulation — Europe.    I. Moran,
Michael.    II. Prosser, Tony.    III. Series.
HD4139.P763  1994
338.94 — dc20                                              93-30284
                                                              CIP

Typeset by Colset Private Limited, Singapore
Printed in Great Britain by St Edmundsbury Press,
Bury St Edmunds, Suffolk

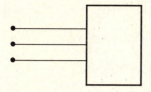

# CONTENTS

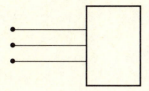

# THE CONTRIBUTORS

*Sabino Cassese* is Director of the Institute of Public Law at the University of Rome, 'La Sapienza'. He was a member of the Policy Unit of the Italian Prime Minister, 1988–9, and since April 1993 has been Minister for the Civil Service in the Cabinet of the Italian Government.

*Michal du Vall* is Professor of Law at the University of Krakow.

*Kenneth Hanf* teaches public administration at Erasmus University, Rotterdam.

*Jeremy Leaman* teaches German politics at the University of Loughborough.

*Tadeusz Markowski* teaches environmental planning at the University of Lodz.

*Michael Mejstřík* works in the Centre for Economic Research and Graduate Education, Charles University, Prague.

*Michael Moran* is Professor of Government at the University of Manchester.

*Istvan Pogany* teaches law at the University of Warwick.

*Tony Prosser* is Professor of Public Law at the University of Glasgow.

*Milan Sojka* teaches economics at the Institute of Economic Sciences, Charles University, Prague

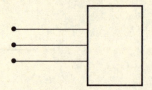

# ACKNOWLEDGEMENTS

The origins of this volume lie in a study group sponsored by the European Community Studies Association, and part funded by the Commission of the the EC. We are grateful for their support. We also thank our contributors for their patience in the face of our numerous editorial demands.

Michael Moran
Tony Prosser

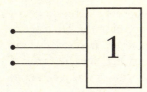

# INTRODUCTION: POLITICS, PRIVATIZATION AND CONSTITUTIONS

## Michael Moran and Tony Prosser

The market was a key word of the 1980s, and in a large number of states the attempt to create and to strengthen market forces was the dominant feature of political life. The ubiquity of the movement to marketize was astonishing: it encompassed old and declining capitalist nations, such as the United Kingdom; vigorous capitalist economies with strong traditions of regulation, such as Germany; and most famously of all, the former command economies of the Communist world.

The movement to strengthen markets is, of course, partly economic in origin and in consequence, but it is more than that. In its most radical forms, marketization has also involved privatization: and this in turn means a wholesale change in the form of property relations and in the relations between markets and ideas. In short, to the economic dimension of change is added a political and a constitutional dimension.

This collection of essays is largely concerned with exploring the relationship between the economic, the political and the constitutional in the process of privatization and marketization. It is comparative in form for a particular reason. The modern history of the movement to marketize and privatize meant that some capitalist nations emerged as leaders and innovators in the process. In particular, the Thatcherite revolution in the United Kingdom meant that, for once, here was an area of economic life where the British emerged as modern pioneers. The example of the Thatcherite experience has proved to be immensely influential internationally. In particular, after the momentous events that led to the collapse of Communism across Eastern Europe at the end of the 1980s, there was intense interest in the Thatcherite achievement on the part of the new administrations in Eastern Europe intent on transforming their economies along capitalist lines. 'Learning' from the Western experience, and especially that of Britain, was a common motivation.

Our intention in this volume is to assess just how far such a process of learning is possible. We have sought to put side by side accounts of privatization and deregulation in some of the leading capitalist economies in Western Europe, together with accounts of the experience of the parallel process in some of the most important of the former command economies. The lessons of these chapters are very clear, but it is as well to state them here. The possibility of learning in the sense of copying is limited; the scale of the changes being attempted in Eastern Europe so dwarf what has been achieved even in Britain that any simple transfer of lessons is unlikely; the process of privatization, while it undoubtedly revolutionizes what may be called the economic constitutions of societies, should not be equated with the advance of market forces in any simple sense; and the Western European experience, notably the extraordinary British achievement under Thatcherism, is closely connected to particular characteristics and conditions unique to specific national settings. This does not mean that learning is impossible, but it does mean identifying which elements in a particular case are peculiar, and therefore unlikely to be reusable in other circumstances.

## THE SCALE OF CHANGE IN EASTERN EUROPE

The detailed case studies of the East European experience in the following chapters examine particular countries. It is, however, worth beginning with a summary of the scale of the revolution that is presently being attempted in the former Communist systems. These changes amount to more than a new *economic* settlement, though they are indeed that; they also involve a new *constitutional/political* settlement. The economic and constitutional settlements are connected. In the economic sphere two key sets of changes are in the process of being put into effect: a programme of privatization (the transfer of ownership from state hands to private agents); and a programme of regulatory reform (chiefly involving the attempt to remove barriers to competition in a wide range of product and labour markets). The contributions by Mejstřík and Sojka, by Du Vall, and by Pogany focus on privatization; that by Markowski focuses on regulatory reform. The best known part of the constitutional settlement involves, of course, the reconstruction of political institutions modelled, in some degree, on the institutions of liberal democracy. But the economic changes also impinge on constitutional reform. Regulatory reform amounts to an attempt to recast the economic constitution – to redesign the rules governing accountability and control in markets. More directly still, the privatization process raises issues that are central to constitutional change. These issues include the relations that are to exist between the State and newly privatized enterprises; the degree, if any, to which privatized enterprises are to be held accountable for their operations; and the institutions to be used in actually accomplishing privatization in the first place.

Some idea of the revolutionary scale of privatization and deregulation may be gathered from Figure 1.1, which compares the size of the State sector in a range of economies in 1991. The figure may be taken as a direct measure of the extent of the privatization task awaiting any government that attempts to shift the former command economies to a market model. It may also be taken as a proxy measure of the scale of any 'deregulation' exercise. We do not have accurate indicators of the comparative extent to which different economies are 'regulated' – subject to State controls short of actual ownership. We know that there are some where a small State sector goes with a high level of regulation. It is recognized, for instance, that the tiny American

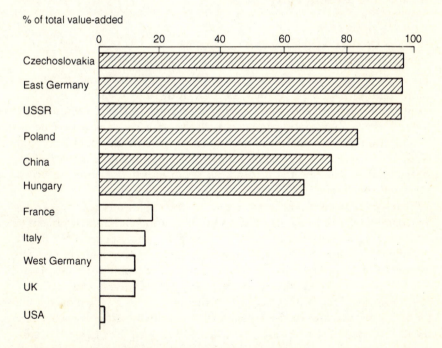

*Figure 1.1*   Share of state sector in selected economies.

*Source*: *Independent*, 7 July 1991

proportions revealed in the chart are not a good measure of the significance of public control in the US economy, because on the other side of the Atlantic regulation has been a substitute for public ownership. Nevertheless, when we look at the economies with an overwhelmingly predominant State sector, such as the Czech case, we are also almost certainly also looking at economies where regulation and control is at a generally high level (although many of these controls were evaded by the extensive black markets). In brief, reforming the economies of the old East European block involves more than the daunting task of privatization; it also involves a wholesale dismantling of barriers to competition and the construction of a new regulatory order.

The figure also, however, counsels us against blanket generalizations about a common 'East European' experience. There is certainly a huge gap between the size of the State sector in the market economics of Western Europe and in the former 'command' economies; but the figure also shows that not all of the latter have experienced State economic domination to the same degree. Indeed, the detailed studies of individual countries in the chapters that follow show that variety, both of problems and of starting point, is a recurrent feature.

## LEARNING FROM COMPARISON?

The scale of the task facing those attempting to marketize and privatize in Eastern Europe lures policy-makers into an obvious temptation: to look elsewhere for lessons about how to privatize. Since by the end of the 1980s some Western European economies had almost a decade's experience of privatization it is natural to ask how far those experiences could be used to guide later privatizers. The temptation to learn by comparing is particularly strong when examining the British case because of the scale of the British privatization effort.

That some lessons can he learnt is evident; but the lessons and the learning are complex. There is plainly much to be understood about the problems of privatization by reflection on the West European, and especially the British experience. Britain is particularly important, because it has had a large scale, pioneering and – judged by what has actually been shifted to the private sector – an unprecedentedly successful programme (Dunsire, 1990). But one of the lessons of the British case is that there are limits to learning – limits set by the peculiarities of the British setting and by the differences between the scale of the British task and what is being attempted elsewhere. Recognizing the unusual nature of the British case, and the limited extent to which it can be straightforwardly copied, is an important part of any learning process.

The British privatiztion programme is an astonishing achievement – whether it is viewed as a catastrophe or as a major contribution to the creation of a more efficient and accountable economy in the United Kingdom. It is a source of astonishment for three reasons: its scale, its scope, and the fact that it was achieved in a democratic political system.

The British case is important not only because of the scale of the programme, but also because of its international impact. Britain has become a world leader in privatization. The achievements of British governments since 1979 are widely admired in the former command economies. The expertise in privatization built up by firms in the nation's financial capital, the City of London, has itself been the basis for a considerable consultancy industry. There is hardly a country in the world that has not drawn on this expertise in formulating and implementing its own privatization programme. Understanding the particular circumstances of the British case is vital, therefore, in order that the exact nature of the achievement be understood and its lessons properly applied.

A glance at Table 3.2 in the British case study contained in Chapter 3 (p. 38), which charts the main landmarks in British privatization since the election of the first Thatcher Administration in 1979, gives some sense of how unusual the British achievement has been. The measures suggested by that table, impressive though they are, do not give a full account of the scale of what has been accomplished. Hardly any major public enterprises remain, and beyond the dramatic privatizations signalled by large-scale Stock Exchange flotations, there have been some private sales. More significantly, a large part of the housing stock has gradually been transferred from the local government ownership to former tenants: in the early years of Thatcherism during the 1980s around one million dwellings were sold (at a large discount on open market prices) (McMahon, 1987). But what even these supplemented figures fail to convey is the unexpected scope of the programme, especially in its later phases. A glance at the table shows that privatization has now extended to public utilities – enterprises once thought of as natural monopolies belonging naturally to the public domain. It has also reached into areas at the core of government: for instance the management of property services and the manufacture of armaments. What the British experience has shown is that, in the face of a determined government, almost nothing is incapable of being privatized. Why have the British managed to push outward the limits of what is capable of being privatized? We here summarize briefly arguments that are developed at greater length in Chapter 3.

Democratic governments are not normally associated with 'heroic' policy transformations. In the case of Britain, in particular, it was conventional wisdom until recently that the policy process was associated with 'muddling through' – with compromise and piecemeal policy change.

The Thatcherite achievement was made possible by a mixture of constitutional and economic conditions. The constitutional framework in the United Kingdom conferred a unique freedom on governments in the privatization process. In other large West European states, such as France and Germany, a written constitution entrenched rights behind special majorities or special institutions. These rights limited both the range of enterprises that could be disposed of, and restricted the freedom of government in terms of methods of disposal and valuation. By contrast, in Britain there are no constitutionally entrenched property rights, which elsewhere raise problems of restitution of nationalized property. Moreover, governments are virtually unconstrained by legal restrictions in making decisions about the values to be placed on public assets, and the methods used for their disposal. In other words, one of the most important conditions for the British privatization 'success' was the extraordinary freedom British constitutional arrangements conferred on ministers intent on making privatization work.

The economic conditions were provided by the organization of British financial markets. Britain has an almost uniquely 'efficient' Stock Market. As a leading world financial centre, London is endowed with the ideal institutional apparatus for large-scale stock flotations: in London there is a concentration of commercial legal skill, underwriting facilities and market making resources perhaps unmatched anywhere outside the United States (Ingham, 1984). How far the combination of a huge and innovative financial centre with a declining, backward industrial base is a healthy combination for the British economy at large is a matter of some dispute. But it indubitably provided the ideal conditions for the heroic scale of British privatizations in the 1980s.

Many of the features that allowed privatization to take place on such a scale have also contributed to the problems of the British privatization experience. Four merit emphasis: valuation and restitution; accountability; competitiveness; and the problem of reconciling the aims of the national government with its international, especially its European, obligations.

On valuation there have been persistent problems in striking a 'fair price' in the disposal of public assets to the private sector. These difficulties are bound up with polemical debates in Britain – for instance, with allegations that undervaluation has been used as a tool by ministers to guarantee 'successful' privatization (i.e. privatization in which there is excess demand for stakes in the privatized concern). But at the root of the difficulty lies the absence of constitutional restraints on governments in making decisions about valuations in the disposal process. In France, by contrast, the Constitutional Council required independent valuation of enterprises being sold. In Central and Eastern Europe, moreover, constitutional rights to property nationalized by the communist regimes have complicated the privatization process – as our chapters on the Czech and Hungarian experience illustrate.

Accountability has been, and remains, a serious problem in the British privatization process. One of the most important lessons of the privatization experience in Britain is that selling an enterprise to the private sector does not mean an end to questions about public control and accountability (Prosser, 1989). Most of the privatized industries are major concerns whose operations have a significant social and economic impact. Some are utilities that still operate as monopolies. No democratic government could possibly neglect the impact such enterprises have on the wider society. In many cases privatization has been accompanied by the creation of an elaborate structure of regulation (for instance in telecommunications); in almost all cases regulatory issues have commanded attention. 'Privatization', therefore, is not so much a retreat by the State, as a shift in the modes of intervention from ownership to regulation. In Britain this shift to regulation has taken place in a country where there is little discussion of the principles on which regulation should take place.

The problem of accountability and regulation impinges on the third problem, which concerns competitiveness. The polemical case for privatization has rested on the claim that privately-owned enterprises are more efficient and competitively responsive than are publicly-owned enterprises. Systematic investigation, as distinct from casual observation of particular examples, suggests a more complex picture. The balance of efficiency and competition between enterprises is affected by a wide range of forces, of which form of ownership is only one. Studies have found cases of both effective and ineffective public sector concerns (Grant and Nath, 1984). But in Britain the polemical equation of privatization with more efficiency and competitiveness has often meant that the two issues – form of ownership and competitive efficiency – have not been disentangled. In important instances privatization has meant the replacement of a public sector monopoly by a private sector monopoly, with the issues of competitiveness unresolved.

The international dimension of privatization is too often neglected. In the British case, membership of the European Community is challenging one of the most distinctive features of the British privatization programme as identified above – the unusual degree to which governments intent on privatization can act in an unfettered way. Three important factors may be observed.

### Competition and transparency

In the field of public utilities there is an emphasis on liberalization of markets, and making relations between governments and utilities more open, which may result in a regulatory style different from that previously adopted in Britain.

*State aids and valuation*

The freedom of British governments to use public subsidies or write-offs to make particular enterprises more attractive candidates for privatization is in direct conflict with Community restrictions on the terms under which State aids can be given to enterprises. The most striking illustration of this occurred in the case of the sale of the Rover Group to British Aerospace, where the Commission has challenged the legitimacy of debt write-offs. The most significant impact of the Commission's intervention may lie less in the substantive impact on valuation policy and more on the process by which decisions are made. It is difficult to see the Government so lightly entering into the sort of secret deals that marked the Rover case in any future privatization. This links directly to the third impact of European Community membership.

*The policy process*

The policy process in Britain generally is marked by informality and secrecy. The privatization policy process has, not surprisingly, also exhibited these features. Membership of the Community is bringing Britain under the influence of very different institutional and legal traditions: traditions in which administrative law is a highly developed discipline and an important influence on the way government conducts itself; traditions in which legal standards are common; traditions in which, consequently, courts are important actors in the policy process in their own right. This will have important consequences for the future regulation of privatized enterprises in the United Kingdom: it will enforce more transparency in relations, require the more exact specification of standards and, probably, make the actors in regulation more litigious.

We have dwelt at some length on the British case both because of the objective scale of the transformation and because of the reputation enjoyed by the British in Eastern Europe. British 'successes' and 'failures' in privatization have much to do with certain unique British attributes – attributes that other nations might not wish to copy, even if copying were possible. The two most obvious contributions lie in the financial markets and in the constitutional sphere. Britain's financial markets are unique – notably in the extraordinarily developed character of her stock markets, which are adept at organizing privatization sales. In addition, the unwritten British constitution, which sets no domestic juridical authority over Parliament, has given ministers a unique freedom in deciding strategy and tactics in the privatization process.

The peculiarities of the British are reinforced by the two other case studies in this volume of the state of privatization and deregulation in major capitalist economies. Leaman's study of Germany shows powerful institutional and economic inhibitions to the privatization process; Cassese shows that Italy has barely set out on the road travelled for so long by Britain.

Similar conclusions could be drawn from a study of the French privatization experience, which has not been included in this volume as detailed coverage is available elsewhere (Graham and Prosser, 1991), and because the fresh round of privatization announced in 1993 should provide further lessons too late for inclusion here.

## BEYOND PRIVATIZATION: DEREGULATION AND REGULATORY REFORM

It is obvious that the replacement of the old command systems by market economies means more than changing forms of ownership; it means abolishing a wide range of restrictions under which economic exchanges formerly took place. In the capitalist economies of Western Europe and the Anglo-Saxon world the 1980s was the decade of deregulation. Thus, while the scope of the task in Eastern Europe is unprecedented, there is ample experience of the problem of trying to abolish restrictions on market entry, on pricing and on other forms of competition. Hardly a major industry or sector has escaped these changes in the 1980s. They have been particularly marked in financial services, where a world-wide revolution in competitive conditions has taken place, in transportation and in telecommunications (Khoury, 1990). To summarize these changes as 'deregulation' would be misleading.

The most important limit to 'deregulation' concerns its significance for the role of government. It would be natural to assume that deregulation meant a retreat by the State. In practice in many sectors the decade of deregulation actually meant an increase in State control over markets. The most striking instance of this is provided by the financial services sector, perhaps the archetypically 'deregulating' sector in the advanced market economies. During the 1980s most of the advanced industrial nations actually passed legislation to increase control over the conduct of business in financial markets (Moran, 1991). In the field of environmental regulation the decade also saw a period of regulatory change rather than of simple deregulation. Why was this?

The most important reason is that deregulation has been used to summarize a wide variety of changes in both the institutions of regulation and in the substantive rules. In some cases reform has indeed involved retreat by the State; in others, it has required the creation of new institutions and the development of newly elaborated rules. The sources of that regulatory reform are threefold, and these three sources may come into conflict with each other.

### The search for international harmonization

Environmental policy, the subject of two case studies in this volume, is only the most obvious instance of a policy arena where it has become clear that policies pursued independently by separate national sovereign entities are of limited use. In this area the role and influence of the institutions of the European Community are at their height.

### The search for effective policy delivery

The spur behind reform in the field of environmental regulation is most commonly the desire to regulate more effectively, rather than the desire to withdraw from regulation.

### The search for 'soft' regulation

By the end of the 1970s the perception had been widely established that traditional, hierarchical, command forms of regulation were suffering from overload. The systems being regulated were so complex, and changing so rapidly, that control was limited, ineffective and prone to breakdown. Environmental regulation is only the most striking example of how these perceptions have led to the search for regulatory instruments that rely less on command and surveillance, and more on inducing the regulated to conform to prescribed standards. The best known of these instruments are the so-called 'market instruments': e.g. 'licences to pollute' or 'polluter pays' principles. But the search for soft regulation involves a recognition of a social reality that is too often neglected in the debates about privatization and deregulation: that there are social institutions, and modes of regulation, other than the market and the State. In reconstructing economies, therefore, policy-makers have a wider choice than the simple dichotomy of State command or market incentive; indeed, if reform is to succeed in Eastern Europe, the example of the market economies of Western Europe suggests that something more than the market is needed. The significance of these regulatory developments is explored at length in Hanf's contribution to this book.

## PROBLEMS OF PRIVATIZATION AND DEREGULATION:
## THE EAST EUROPEAN EXPERIENCE

The case studies of change in the old command economies recounted in this book allow us to draw no simple generalizations. On the contrary, they emphasize two features: the variety of experiences presently being undergone in Eastern Europe; and the rapidly changing character of the economic and political systems where reform is being attempted. Even State structures and boundaries are not stable: the writing of the Czechoslovak case has, most obviously, been overtaken by the 'velvet divorce' – the agreement of the Slovak and the Czech Republics to dissolve the federation. The diverse experiences often have deep historical roots; take, for example, the Polish and the Czech cases. Polish interest in dismantling the old command economy is much more firmly established; the Czech reforms only became conceivable after the extraordinary events of late 1989. Economically the two systems are also very different: parts of the former Czechoslovakia have a history of successful industrialization that predates Communist rule. Finally, the main part of Polish agriculture has always been in private hands.

Despite these differences, however, a reflection on the content of the individual case studies suggests that the former command economies face common problems. These problems may be summarized as institutional, structural and political.

### Institutional problems

It is obvious from a consideration of the British privatizations – measures far less ambitious than those now contemplated in Eastern Europe – that the success of those measures depended on a particular institutional configuration. Among the most important features of this configuration were: a highly developed capital market; an elaborate jurisprudence provided by company law and labour law; a particular constitutional tradition that allowed rapid solutions to technical problems like the valuation of assets, and that conferred freedom to offer assets for sale unhindered by claims for restitution; and a unitary constitutional structure. All of these have to be invented, virtually from nothing, in the former command economies. Even Hungary, the most 'marketized' of the economies before the collapse of Communism, has securities markets that, by British standards, are rudimentary. The shortage of capital is only the most obvious deficiency. It is not enough to privatize concerns; a functioning market economy will require an appropriate network of rules and institutions governing the relations between companies and their creditors, their customers and their employees.

### Structural problems

The command economies collapsed, in part, because they were inefficient. The command system hid a huge under-utilization of labour. Exposure to even a small dose of market discipline will force large-scale shedding of labour. Privatization, unless it involves the recreation of a private sector monopoly, necessarily leads to large-scale closures and unemployment, especially in heavy industry. The case of Hungary is again instructive, precisely because its position is perhaps the strongest of all those considered here: of the 450 firms originally founded by the Hungarian Ministry of Industry and Trade as State-owned companies, 102 have filed for bankruptcy. The ministry forecasts a final figure of 150 bankruptcies, which would amount to a 33 per cent cut in production and the loss of some 130,000 jobs. This connects in a very obvious way to political problems.

### Political problems

Some of the British privatizations – notably in traditional heavy industry – were also associated with the closure of inefficient concerns. It is also widely accepted that some drastic closure programmes in industries presently publicly owned – notably coal-mining – are a prelude to privatization. These structural changes have involved immensely difficult tasks of political management, to cope with social unrest and resistance from those made redundant, or threatened with redundancy. That task of political management proved problematic even in a democracy as soundly based, and a political culture as consensual, as exists in Britain. The problems inherent in the political management of economic turbulence and deprivation in political systems where democratic institutions and political consensus are both new and fragile creations hardly needs labouring.

## CONCLUSION

All research has an interim quality: any conclusions must be tentative, allowing the possibility of falsification by subsequent evidence. But the provisional character of social observation is nowhere more clearly demonstrated than in the subject of this book. In particular in the case of the old command economies we are trying to make sense of hugely radical reforms, at the start of their lives, in conditions of great economic and political uncertainty. In the West European case relatively settled constitutional arrangements, and relatively well established institutions and social forces, shape the outcomes of regulatory reform; no such boundaries constrain outcomes on the other side of the old Iron Curtain divide. But difficult though it is to make sense of rapidly changing social events, social enquiry cannot afford to postpone investigation and debate until outcomes are settled. We have to try to make sense of developments as they take place, however bewildering those events may be. It is in the spirit of such provisional enquiry that the cases in this book are offered.

# BIBLIOGRAPHY

Dunsire, A. (1990) The public-private debate: some United Kingdom evidence, *International Review of Administrative Science*, 56(1), 29–61.

Graham, C. and Prosser, T. (1991) *Privatizing Public Enterprises*. Oxford, Clarendon.

Grant, W. and Nath, S. (1984) *The Politics of Economic Policymaking*. Oxford, Blackwell.

Ingham, G. (1984) *Capitalism Divided: The City and Industry in British Social Development*. London, Macmillan.

Khoury, S. (1990) *The Deregulation of the World Financial Markets: Myths, Realities and Impact*. New York, Quorum.

McMahon, P. (1987) The sale of local authority houses in Britain, *Geography*, 6(1), 169–71.

Moran, M. (1991) *The Politics of the Financial Services Revolution*. London, Macmillan.

Prosser, T. (1989) Regulation of privatized enterprises: institutions and procedures. In L. Hancher and M. Moran (eds) *Capitalism, Culture and Economic Regulation*. Oxford, Clarendon Press.

# 2

# REGULATORY REFORM AND PRIVATIZATION IN GERMANY

## Jeremy Leaman

### SETTING THE DEREGULATION AGENDA

Germany is the undisputed economic leader of Europe. Its economic virtues, however, have been increasingly interpreted as potential sources of weakness: a high export ratio as dangerous export dependency (Glastetter *et al.*, 1983; Leaman 1988), secular economic and structural political continuities as potential 'policy immobilism' (Bulmer and Humphreys, 1989), social stability as fiscally unsustainable levels of provision, etc. Against the background of global economic instability, Germany has been seen as a prime candidate for structural reforms of one kind or another. What shape these modifications take, is the subject of fierce political debate; deregulation is the banner adopted by neo-liberals in that debate.

The relationship between State and economy in Germany, which lies at the heart of the deregulation agenda, has indeed become increasingly critical in recent years; sluggish domestic demand, growth rates below the Organization for Economic Cooperation and Development (OECD) average in the 1970s and early 1980s, demographic imbalances, the persistence of mass unemployment and increasing State deficits have all remained largely resistant to the Keynesian, monetarist and supply-side programmes which the German guardians of the 'social market' had adopted since the late 1960s. The key elements of orthodox (non-governmental) thinking in the 1970s and early 1980s were rooted in perceptions of the distributional conflict between capital and labour and between capital and the State, stressing the macro-economic costs of a rising wages ratio and the crowding-out effects of State borrowing (viz. Biedenkopf and Miegel, 1979). The Council of Economic Experts (*Sachverständigenrat*), purged of Keynesianism, consistently urged wage restraint and a roll-back of State activity; as early as 1975 the Academic Sub-Committee of the Federal Finance Ministry proposed privatization as a means of reducing public deficits (Goldberg, 1988: 254).

The perception of a rising wages ratio, a rising State ratio and a rising State borrowing requirement are objectively correct (Glastetter *et al.*, 1983) and can certainly be used to illustrate arguments of a latent fiscal crisis or latent distributional crisis. However, the arguments of many neo-liberal critics of the social-liberal coalition in Bonn (which governed from 1969 to 1982) were extremely selective, ignoring important structural deficiencies in Germany's economic constitution, above all the distorting effects of monopolies and monopsonies (concentrated demand) on markets, and the structural political weakness of the federal government in the face of a dominant independent *Bundesbank*. The premature demise of Helmut Schmidt's government and the ushering-in of Helmut Kohl's *Wende* (great change) in 1982 has in fact been ascribed to *Bundesbank* pressure (Kennedy, 1991).

The supply-side rhetoric of the *Wende* called for a return to State probity, dynamic entrepreneurialism and export-led growth. The Stuttgart Principles of the Christian Democratic Union (CDU) highlighted the need for enhanced international competitiveness and identified scope for deregulating planning law and for privatizating State holdings and enterprises. Greatest stress, however, is placed on the liberalization of the labour market (CDU, 1984a). The control of economic concentration, the central pillar of the CDU's 1949 Düsseldorf Principles and the architecture of Erhard's 'social market economy', gets barely a passing mention in the the CDU's 1984 programme dedicated though it is to the 'renewal of the social market economy' (CDU, 1984b).

The movement towards deregulation in Germany was accelerated by particular international factors: currency deregulation in 1972 introduced new uncertainties into global systems of exchange and demanded at the very least national regulatory adaptation to the new circumstances; international competitiveness had been made more acute by the increased costs of imported energy; furthermore, the apparent employment potential of deregulation, as practised in the United States by the Reagan Administration, began to raise hopes in Europe of tackling the electoral burden of mass unemployment with similar measures; thus the 1986 Single European Act (SEA) marks the formal response of the European Commission (EC) to both the danger of intensified competition and the promise of the removal/standardization of European market regulation. Within Germany there was an extensive campaign by industry and its allies from 1987 onwards, focusing on the decreasing attractiveness of the country as a location (*Standort*) for investment. It stressed high tax rates, high wages, high energy costs and high environmental costs as features of an over-regulated economy (Institut der dentschen Wirtschift [IW hereafter], 1988).

In March 1987, Chancellor Kohl announced the formation of an 'independent commission of experts for the reduction of regulations incompatible with the market'. The commission began its work a year later under the chairmanship of Jürgen Donges, submitting an interim report in March 1990 and a final report in March 1991 (Deregulierungskommission [DK hereafter], 1991). Meanwhile the Monopoly Commission, in its main report for 1986/7, stressed the potential for deregulating the insurance sector and of reforming company law (Monopolkommission, 1988).

The deregulation agenda set by federal government ministries and the Federal Cartel Office represented a universal programme, embracing general features of the political economy such as company law, mergers, public procurement and technical standards as well as individual sectors of the economy, from transport and telecommunications through to housing and financial services. The language of that programme is radically neo-liberal, implying a widescale dismissal of Germany's inherited regulatory culture. The latter is characterized graphically in terms of 'sclerosis' (Merklein, 1985), 'encrustation' and 'ossification' (DK 1991: 1). Such negative vocabulary is supported in the Deregulation Commission's report by its account of the origins of German regulation – 'largely the fruit of the economic crisis of the 1930s' – and by its definition of regulation as 'every State or State-sanctioned restriction of a person's opportunities for action and disposition' (DK, 1991: 1). The association of State regulation with the Depression and Nazism is both misleading and indeed unnecessary for presenting the intellectual case for regulatory reform; likewise the negative definition that counterposes regulatory restrictions with individual freedom. The historicity of (capitalist) State forms and their regulatory statutes is self-evident, the justification of a 'constant need for revision' (DK, 1991: 6f) unexceptionable. The problems arise, however, when this banality is elevated to the level of fundamentalist theology, which confuses the part – the appropriateness of regulatory revisions in given areas – with the whole – over-regulation as the single source of economic deficiencies, deregulation therefore as 'the model of an economic policy directed to the future' (DK, 1991: V; see also OECD, 1988).

Germany's deregulation programme has been flanked by fiscal supply-side measures (tax reforms and *planned* subsidy cuts) and by tight monetary policy (Arbeitsgruppe Alternative Wirtschaftpolitik [AAW hereafter], 1991). Woolcock, Hodges and Schreiber distinguish between 'market-led' and 'policy-led' measures of regulatory reform (Woolcock *et. al.*, 1991), i.e. measures determined by compulsion or by choice. The bulk of German 'policy-led' deregulation and privatization measures up to 1992 have been directed at the labour market, at conditions of employment and at the reduction of social provision (housing, health) as well as to improved fiscal balances; most others have either been 'market-led', like the liberalization of securities markets, or dictated by the SEA and other EC harmonization programmes, for example in the case of public procurement contracts. Much of the remaining deregulation agenda is still at the planning or consultation phase. Yet further areas of concern, notably competition policy, have been given at most minimal priority. Despite the missionary appeal of deregulation as a universal programme, therefore, certain areas have been given priority. The survey that follows will therefore concentrate on key areas of regulatory reform and privatization: labour market deregulation, because it lies at the heart of supply-side policies in Germany, the reform of securities markets, because this reflects critical features of capital valorization in a changing global environment, public procurement and competition policies, and federal privatization measures. In conclusion there will be a critical assessment of the overall programme, including the prospects of further deregulation.

## THE DEREGULATION OF LABOUR

The Deregulation Commission's recommendations on labour market deregulation echo very closely those of the OECD (OECD, 1990b: 23) but they come on top of a decade of secular and regulatory changes to the labour market. The implications of the campaign are far-reaching.

Within the OECD the German economy is marked by generally high wage levels, high levels of training and skill, high labour productivity, the shortest working year, highly juridified industrial relations, mandatory social insurance, high levels of employment and social protection and (not unrelatedly) high levels of social stability. The rules governing working rights have been accumulated gradually over more than a century of reforming legislation. Their funding and implementation involve considerable public costs (namely German Labour Courts and training establishments) and high marginal wage costs in the order of 84 per cent (1987) of direct wage costs (GB: 42 per cent, US: 37 per cent, Japan: 29 per cent) (IW, 1988).

The standard justification for extensive regulation of labour markets is their *unique character compared to other commodity markets*. Some proponents of deregulation deny the validity of this distinction and plead for its suspension (Keuchel, 1989; Besters, 1990). The DK concedes it (DK, 1991: 137), but nevertheless defines 'the regulation in the labour market' negatively as one that 'largely suspends competition', making 'cartel agreements the rule' (DK, 1991: 136). Furthermore, it is clear both from the DK's diagnosis and prescriptions that the distinction should be radically revised, since the 'workers question' of the nineteenth century 'is no longer valid', 'under-cutting-competition' among the wage-dependent does not take place and there is demand from workers themselves for 'the individualization of working relations' (DK, 1991: 138).

The argument matches the long-standing critique by employers' organizations of immoderate wage demands, high marginal wage costs and the extravagance of the social state, which was mirrored in state crisis management policies of the last two and a half decades. The common logic of these policies runs: labour moderation equals lower business costs equals higher profits equals higher investment equals higher growth equals increased employment. Accordingly the rise in the wages ratio in the 1970s implied the need to reduce union power and relieve corporate costs. It also implied that the regulatory culture of labour was dysfunctional for the interests of capital.

Mass unemployment, which continued to rise after the 1981/82 recession, altered labour market conditions fundamentally such that real wages and the gross wages ratio continued to fall throughout the 1980s (1980: 65 per cent; 1988: 59 per cent), while profits and the profits ratio rose. Whether by accident or design unemployment became a powerful secular lever for a series of regulatory reforms by the federal governments.

- The Early Retirement Law (1984) made firms eligible for grants from the Federal Agency for Labour towards early retirement packages, but only at the firm's request and not at that of the individual employee.
- The 1984 revision of the Youth Employment Protection Law modified certain requirements governing the deployment of apprentices, giving employers greater flexibility (cf. AAW 1989; 69).
- The 1985 law governing The Social Plan in Bankruptcy and Insolvency Proceedings on the one hand confirmed the primacy of the 'social plan' (covering severance pay, etc.) before other creditors' claims but limited individual compensation to the equivalent of only 2.5 monthly salaries and the total volume of social plan funds to one third of residual assets.
- The hitherto deepest inroads into labour law were achieved by the 1985 Employment Promotion Law: a) opportunities for short-term contracts of employment were increased by extending the maximum contract period from 6 to 18 months (24 months in new businesses); b) subcontracted labour regulations were modified, allowing six-month contracts instead of the previous three; c) the trigger threshold of redundancies at which Works Councils had the right to insist on social plan arrangements was almost doubled.
- In 1986 the (by European standards) restrictive Shop Closing Act was liberalized, extending potential working hours for certain shop workers.

- Strike laws were altered in 1986, removing benefit entitlement from third parties in a union affected by the regional strike action of union colleagues; in the same year, the Law for the Disabled removed the six-month special protection from dismissal for newly employed disabled workers.
- Maritime law was altered in 1989, allowing German registered ships to employ foreign sailors at rates of pay obtaining in their country of origin.

There is some disagreement over the quantitative impact of these deregulation measures. The OECD, which has campaigned strongly for worldwide deregulation, notes 'comparatively little progress' in labour deregulation (OECD, 1988), while a number of academics close to the German trade unions have stressed the 'enormous redistribution in favour of profits in the course of the 1980s' resulting from the combined effect of mass unemployment and labour deregulation (Müller and Seiffert, 1991), to the 'erosion of the normal labour relationship' (Däubler, 1988) and to specific effects of short-term contracts on employment in the expanding service sector, such that over 50 per cent of all employment was now 'unprotected' by standard provisions of protection (Möller, 1988). On the other hand there is no evidence to suggest that the measures produced any significant increase in employment to compensate for the 'increased instability of employment' (Müller and Seiffert, 1991; Dombois, 1989).

The Deregulation Commission makes twelve proposals for further labour deregulation in its 1991 report: these include measures allowing the temporary suspension of collective wage agreements, the extension of short-term contracts from 18 to 36 months, the liberalization of sub-contracted labour, greater flexibility in dismissal regulations, and limitations on or even the suspension of social plan provisions. The section on the labour market concludes with a statement stressing the supply-side and cost advantages of such liberalization:

> The Federal Republic as a location for production and investment will be enhanced in international competition because, with a more efficient labour market, mobile capital can reckon on a more attractive rate of return. It is not true that employees need be acutely concerned about their chances of employment through deregulation and reregulation; if increasing numbers of workers are dismissed, the chances of re-employment in a well functioning labour market are greater than in one which is excessively regulated.
>
> (DK 1991: 157)

Heinz Markmann's minority vote in the Commission's report reflects the general tenor of the opposition to the proposals for further labour market deregulation: that they are intellectually sloppy and economically dangerous. Markmann, the former head of WSI, the trade union research institute, reasserts the structural subordination of labour to capital in every market economy, which is denied or trivialized by the majority group but which has been the historical basis for labour market regulations, and claims that the weakening of established rules will increase the structural dominance of employers as 'monopsonistic' agents in the labour market without achieving the desired result of increased employment. Unions were not opposed to modifications of regulations, indeed had demonstrated considerable interest in certain aspects of flexibilization. However, the flexibility afforded by established and proposed changes in labour regulations largely served the interest of employers; above all the 'individualization' of labour contracts represented 'regression to times where there are no collective contracts whatsoever'; the liberalization of the labour market 'breaks the norms of social and economic ethics', while the assumed effects of the process could not be substantiated empirically. 'The psychological, social and political damage, which the deregulation and reregulation measures proposed by the majority would inflict on our community, would be intolerable' (DK, 1991: 157–160; see also Müller and Seiffert, 1991; Hickel, 1991).

The case for labour market deregulation on the grounds of increased allocational efficiency remains unproven. Ernst Fehr and others argue convincingly that labour markets are potentially better served by systems of industrial relations that include strong centralized trade unions, national wage bargaining and high real wages rooted in skills, and that the moves towards plant-level or even individualized contracts have dysfunctional effects on the mobility of labour (Fehr, 1990). On a broader level the research by Lijpart and Crepaz suggests that the macro-economic performance of countries with consensual systems of labour relations is better than the relatively conflict-based systems common in Anglo-Saxon countries (Lijpart and Crepaz, 1991).

## THE DEREGULATION OF FINANCIAL SERVICES

A simplified definition of the function of the financial services sector in a market economy would be the mobilization and allocation of capital to enable and protect risk in other sectors. One author likens this enabling role to that of the medical services (Llewellyn, 1992). There have been considerable historical and national differences in the size of this sector and the degree of interdependence between it and the rest of the economy: the size, strength and international presence of British and American financial services contrast with the relative insularity of the German system. In judging the issue of regulatory reform of the German system, it is therefore essential to assess the structural relationships of the overall national economy as well as the international division of labour between sectorally differing economies.

German financial markets are highly regulated by international standards, but rely on a large measure of self-regulation. The dominant structural feature of these markets is the system of *universal banking*, which combines house-banking and large-scale equity holdings. The system was introduced in the 1850s to compensate for the general weakness of German capital markets and rudimentary stock markets to provide long-term industrial finance. It has since become a key feature of Germany's political economy. The banking sector is dominated by the 'big three' (*Deutsche, Dresdner* and *Commerz*) but supplemented by a considerable network of publicly-owned savings banks (*Sparkassen*), often also operating as universal banks. The universal banks have traditionally dominated equity markets; savings capital is concentrated in deposit accounts and fixed interest securities with limited private share ownership. Small shareholders customarily cede their voting rights to the banks through a well-developed proxy system.

The regulatory culture of German banking is 'comparatively unfettered' (Moran, 1992), the economic power of the big banks prodigious (Pfeiffer, 1989). Liquidity and admission rules were only introduced in 1934 by the Nazis after the banking crash of 1931 and then reshaped in the Credit System Law of 1961, which also created the centralized Supervisory Office for the Credit System in Berlin. Allied plans to outlaw universal banking in the Dodge Plan of 1945 were shelved in favour of deconcentration measures, which were then rapidly reversed in the 1950s. Banking is exempted from the provisions of the 1957 Cartel Law. While there is some support within the *Bundestag* for the tightening of banking regulations, notably in limiting equity holdings in non-banks, and while there have been some calls for the privatization of savings banks, there is no constituency for the abolition of the universal banking principle and little sign of urgent reform legislation; nor was bank deregulation on the agenda of either the Monopolies Commission or the Deregulation Commission. Rather, German banking is seen to be under threat from the global nature of capital markets, from insurance companies diversifying into banking, from securities markets offering cheaper flexible modes of finance, and from EC liberalization of banking, which has allowed foreign banks to compete for savings and credit business in Germany from 1 January 1993 (Moran, 1992; Woolcock *et al.*, 1991).

German banking costs are – relative to rediscount costs – certainly high by European standards, particularly for overdrafts and small businesses (*Der Spiegel*, 22/1991); one EC report has estimated that the liberalization demanded by the SEA should produce a 13 per cent reduction in these costs (European Commission, 1988). There have been a number of minor liberalization measures involving foreign banks in the mid-1980s (see Moran, 1992), although it is unclear whether this has significantly affected the market position of the German big banks. It is equally unclear whether the suspension of competitive barriers will help to dent the German banking fortress, given both the costs and risks involved in establishing new banking networks (Woolcock, 1991) and the conservatism of German savings and credit culture in retail banking.

In contrast to banking, the *insurance sector* has been the object of particular scrutiny by German and European proponents of deregulation. Both the Monopolies and the Deregulation Commission reports make extensive proposals for reform, in part predetermined by EC moves towards opening-up hitherto protected national markets (Woolcock, 1991). German insurance is indeed one of the most highly regulated and protected insurance branches in Europe. The regulatory agency, the *Bundesaufsichtsamt für das Versicherungswesen* (BAV), administers a tight rule book governing admission, liability, type and terms of contract and, up until recently, mandatory specialization (*Spartentrennung*), which forbids the combination of life and general insurance under one roof, ostensibly to protect policyholders, third parties and beneficiaries but, as seems increasingly clear, in fact to protect insurance companies from unwanted competition (Moran, 1992; Woolcock, 1991); reform proposals would shift key regulatory control from the BAV to the Cartel Office. The European Court of Justice has ruled against both BAV (1986) and the Association of German Insurers (1987) in cases involving competition by foreign insurers.

The rigid, prescriptive cartel structure of German insurance – exempt from the cartel provisions of the 1957 Cartel Law – produces bureaucratic inefficiencies, sub-optimal economies of scale and the convenience of price-fixing for premiums. German premiums were found to be consistently above the European average in a recent study: higher than 42 per cent for commercial fire and theft, for example (EC, 1988). With the help of such price advantages the biggest German insurance company, *Allianz*, accumulated huge financial reserves, which it has used to become one of Germany's largest holding companies, with interests in industry and banking. The recent acquisition of 25 per cent of the *Bayersiche Hypothekenbank* and the massive equity swap with the *Dresdner Bank* have made the concept of *Allfinanz* all too real. The *Allianz-Dresdner* case, with a variety of indirect linkages, represents an obvious abuse of German merger law and makes the *Allianz* a rival actor to the universal banks (see *Der Spiegel*, 14/1992).

The insurance lobby succeeded in limiting new German legislation to the implementation of EC directives, despite pressure from the Cartel Office to instigate a more thorough-going reform. As a result only mandatory specialization has been completely abolished for liability and credit insurance, and provisionally suspended for life business, pending a review in 1995. It was predictable that the Deregulation Commission would make additional liberalization proposals for the sector. The most significant is the end of exemption from cartel legislation, except for health and other mandatory insurance. Further proposals include the reduction of mandatory contractual conditions in general insurance, escape clauses for policy-holders, free competition for premiums, liberalization of no-claims arrangements, the replacement of expensive solvency systems by collective protection funds and finally greater access for foreign insurance companies. The insurance sector has already signalled its intention to resist such change.

*Securities exchanges* have played a relatively minor role in the mobilization of capital in Germany's economic history. This is primarily a function of the structural dominance of German banks in the economy and in the financial sector. Apart from their own extensive equity holdings, the universal banks assist in the flotation of shares and bonds, dominate 80 per cent of share trading (Moran, 1989) and vote their depositors' shares as proxies in company AGMs. Only 5 per cent of the population own shares, compared to 18 per cent in the US and 15 to 17 per cent in Britain. Indeed, share ownership by private households fell as a proportion of share capital from 27 per cent in 1960 to 16 per cent in 1982, the bulk (49 per cent) being in the hands of other enterprises and banks (see Moran, 1989). As a result the volume of trading on the nine provincial stock markets in Germany is far lower than in the major financial centres of the world such as London and New York. The bulk of German trading in commodities futures is conducted via the big exchanges in London and Rotterdam or in the US and the Far East, and up until 1990 *financial futures* trading was in large measure illegal.

The German securities sector, 'backward' and parochial as it may be, is (still) an inseparable part of a uniquely integrated productive economy. The key issue would seem to be the degree to which the German financial system serves the allocational needs of the capitalist economy and the degree to which the higher direct costs of retail and wholesale banking are offset by the indirect benefits of long-term financial security for German enterprises. A separate issue is the transparency and 'fairness' in the ownership and disposition of stocks and other securities.

The pressure for the reform of Germany's financial sector has come, in the main, from external market pressures and EC harmonization moves. There has been a small but powerful lobby centred on the Hesse government and the *Bundesbank* to establish a futures exchange in Frankfurt, but there was little urgency at federal level and some resistance from other provincial exchanges and their respective regional governments. The reform of the German Stock Exchange Law in 1989, which finally allowed the establishment of the futures exchange (*Deutsche Terminbörse*) in 1990, has loosened the hold of regional regulators of the system and clearly offers wider options for companies attempting to counteract monetary and currency instability. Equally significant is the fact that the futures exchange is dominated by the big banks both administratively and in volume terms (Moran, 1992). The recent Holding Company Law and the Institutional Investors Law, while designed ostensibly to improve small firms' access to securities markets, also strengthen the structural power of universal banks and insurance companies (AAW, 1988). The abolition of stock exchange turnover tax, effective from January 1991, brings Germany into line with Britain and France and removes a potential disincentive from equity trading.

The proscription of insider trading in shares in Germany is the direct result of the EC directive of November 1989, not of national reforming zeal (Woolcock, 1991). The policing of the directive, however, is left to individual national authorities and this 'leaves open the possibility of a merely symbolic German enforcement regime' (Moran, 1992). This fear is made more plausible by the fact that Germany's shareholding culture is controlled not by an independent network of brokers and market-makers but by a tightly interconnected institutional oligarchy, involving reciprocal parcel holdings by industrial, commercial, banking and insurance enterprises that either makes insider trading superfluous (*qua* indifference to short-term profit-taking) or endemic, given the predominance of out-of-hours trading (Moran, 1989).

The modest deregulation of financial services that has taken place in the late 1980s will remain largely an irrelevance within the German environment unless the key issue of banking power is addressed. There is very little likelihood of this. Rather, there seems a greater likelihood of universal banking becoming more pervasive nationally and internationally, first as German banks gear up for increased international competition through increased takeovers of domestic and foreign banks and second as other countries relax their controls on banking practice, allowing increasingly long-term and large holdings of non-bank equity. This possibility has been reinforced by the EC's Second Banking Coordination Directive, which was adopted in 1989 and took effect in January 1993, which allows German universal banks to operate as such in other EC countries on the basis of German banking regulations. Countries such as Denmark, which have tighter banking regulations but are structurally dependent on Germany, could be forced to legalize universal banking for competing Danish banks.

The auguries for wider share ownership are not very promising (AAW, 1988: 136ff). Recent surveys confirm resistance to share-ownership, particularly among young people (*Der Spiegel*, 5/1990), possibly reinforced by the fact that the Frankfurt exchange showed the highest year-on-year losses in the world after the October 1987 crash.

One important question remains: are the future allocational needs of Germany's economy best served by the bank-led financial sector or by a deregulated European financial services market? There is increasing support for the view that currency deregulation, together with the liberalization of financial services, has produced a 'decoupling' of financial markets from the 'real' economy (Strange, 1986; Altvater, 1992) and that the valorization of capital in financial 'investments' is easier than in productive or commercial investments. The velocity of circulation increases without any corresponding increase in use-values, but interest income is generated at the margin of every transaction. The ratio of share value growth on the Frankfurt stock exchange and general profit growth of 15:1 in 1987 illustrates this de-coupled circulation within the financial sector; equally the ratio of daily global currency transactions ($350 billion) to daily global trade ($17 billion) is over 21:1 (Herr and Voy, 1989). The implication of this trend is that financial services run the risk of ceasing to 'serve' the productive and commercial economy and of undermining real accumulation. While Germany is not and cannot be immune from the influence of global capital market volatility, there is enough evidence to suggest that bank dominance of equity and now futures markets provides a firmer (if oligarchic) basis for resource allocation than a deregulated and radically decoupled financial sector as in Britain. With the globalization of commerce and EC harmonization and liberalization of financial services, German investors will in any case have access to non-German financial markets, thus providing some degree of correction to Germany's huge trade surplus with EC partners like France and Britain. In the absence of global currency reregulation, bank dominance is a guarantee of some economic stability. The case for breaking the cartel structures of German insurance through deregulation and market-opening is very strong, however.[1]

## PUBLIC PROCUREMENT AND COMPETITION POLICY

Public purchasing of goods and services in the EC amounted to 15 per cent of GDP and 32 per cent of all state expenditure in 1987; in Germany the figures were 11.8 per cent and 26.3 per cent respectively (Swann, 1992). The purchasing practice of EC states in this area has been traditionally restrictive, despite EC directives governing public works (1971) and public supply contracts (1977). In 1985 foreign suppliers covered only 4 per cent of German and 0.4 per cent of British public orders (Woolcock, 1991). The restrictions derive from a variety of motives, most notably national and regional economic policies (Swann, 1992) but represent significant (non-tariff) barriers to competition and to the implementation of the SEA. The EC estimates that EC states could save up to 19 billion ECU through liberalizing procurement regulations and practice (Woolcock, 1991). The EC's 1989 Compliance Directive originally envisaged centralized EC monitoring of contracts, with the right to suspend unjustifiable arrangements. This Directive has subsequently been watered down, so that national bodies will be responsible for monitoring and implementing compliance regulations, which in any case only cover contracts in excess of 5 million ECU. There is widespread scepticism about the effectiveness of procurement liberalization measures, despite the apparent fiscal attractions of market-opening. A significant period of grace for the new East German *Länder*, allowing non-compliance to the utilities directives by public bodies up to 1993, has been interpreted accordingly as a chance for German suppliers 'to "sew up", the . . . very large market in investment in the utilities' (Woolcock, 1991).

The scepticism of potential foreign suppliers of national procurement contracts can be seen in part in the wave of cross-national mergers which accelerated in the late 1980s in advance of the implementation of the SEA. The importance of market presence for construction companies led in part to the takeover by Philipp Holzmann AG of NORD FRANCE S.A.; economies of scale arguments have led to a series of cross-national mergers, joint takeovers and equity swaps in the telecommunications sector to ease access into State-dominated telecommunications procurement markets, in part encouraged by both national governments and the EC. The 'strategic alliances' between Siemens and IBM, VW and Ford, Daimler-Benz and Mitsubishi, reflect both economies of scale considerations and a clear desire to avoid (destructive) competition. These developments towards increasing concentration and co-operation have obvious implications for both public procurement deregulation and for competition policy in general.

German and EC merger policy is subject to contradictory pressures: it has to secure free and fair competition in commodity and service markets, preventing excessive market dominance, while at the same time ensuring that German and European enterprises are strong enough to compete on key global export markets. The Berlin Cartel Office and the EC have consistently favoured the international competitiveness argument in assessing mergers, while maintaining the rhetoric of competition and taking selective action against some cartels and some mergers (Leaman, 1988). Recent amendments to German takeover regulations, like the Holding Company Law and the Institutional Investors Law, reinforce concentration and centralization, as noted above. Even when the Cartel Office ruled against the Daimler-Benz-Mitsubishi merger on the grounds of excessive market share, the Economics Minister overruled the ban for reasons of international competitiveness.

Notifiable mergers in Germany virtually tripled from 709 in 1985 to 2,007 in 1991, paralleled by a similar rise in mergers involving Europe's top 1,000 companies (1984/85: 208; 1989/90: 622). The 'merger mania' of the late 1980s reflects a number of trends, including the increasing global nature of markets and the increasing scale economies of high-tech investments. However, a major determinant was the increasing over-accumulation of financial reserves in large corporations (Goldberg, 1988) linked to unregulated world capital markets. The ratio of reserves to fixed assets of German enterprises rose from 70 per cent (1971–5) to 100 per cent in 1990. These reserves facilitated mergers both as speculative operations and as means for conglomerates 'to secure their market positions for as long as possible against market influences from Europe and worldwide' (Kartte, 1992). The record of competition-policing in Germany and Europe, as Cartel Office chief Kartte has frequently conceded, is unimpressive. Future prospects are even less auspicious. Since 1990 it is the EC that assesses all mergers in and between member states involving a combined turnover of more than 5 billion ECU. EC merger law is generally regarded as more permissive than German law, and its interpretation is highly contentious. Kartte, who retired in 1992, stated bluntly that 'there is absolutely no consensus between Sicily and Ireland about what competition policy is supposed to be' (Kartte, 1992). Where competition is supposed to be the cornerstone of deregulation and the SEA, such confusion hardly augurs well.

Globalization and 'single markets' require particular economies of scale for the major actors, of that there is no doubt. Nevertheless, large competitors on global markets remain oligopolies on national, regional and local markets and monopsonies for localized labour and subordinate supplier markets. Public procurement practice will not automatically open up to foreign suppliers just because of supra-national directives, since local and regional prosperity will continue to depend on the virtuous cycle of production, employment and taxation. However, the asymmetry of permissive merger policies and ineffective compliance to new procurement rules could easily increase the structural dependence of local and regional economies on a few oligopolies. A policy mechanism linking procurement, merger and regional policy would allow a more differentiated view of specific local and regional market requirements.

## PRIVATIZATION

In its review of 'structural reform' the OECD acknowledged that 'the scope for privatizations has been much smaller' in Germany than in some other advanced capitalist countries (OECD, 1990b). Privatization of State enterprises and State holdings was nevertheless an important element of the *Wende* programme (CDU, 1984a) and has become a consistent feature of State policy since 1987. Up to the early 1980s privatization had been limited to isolated measures involving local cleaning and environmental services (Goldberg, 1988). The new programme is linked ideologically to deregulation and the roll-back of the State: 'The privatization policy of this government is not determined by fiscal considerations but is primarily a task of policy related to the economic order' (Bundesministerium für Finanzen (BFM), 1987). The measures have therefore been linked to the prospect of wider share ownership, fairer distribution of productive property, market-opening and de-concentration. The evidence to date suggests no such benefits (AAW, 1988: 152ff).

In 1983 the federal state had complete or part holdings in 487 enterprises. The most significant State enterprises (100 per cent or majority share) were in the transport and communications sector: Federal Post, Federal Railways, *Lufthansa*. Significant minority holdings included the energy conglomerate *VEBA* and *Volkswagen*. In addition the federal state owned the *Salzgitter* steel group and the State holding company *VIAG*, among others. Between 1983 and 1989 the federal government sold its entire holding in *VEBA*, *Volkswagen* and *VIAG*, all in three stages; it sold off the whole *Salzgitter* group in 1989, some 10 per cent of *Lufthansa* in 1987, 48 per cent of the *DSL-Bank* in 1989, all of the industrial holding company *DIAG* in 1990 and the entire holding in the *Deutsche Pfandbrief- und Hypothetkenbank* in 1991. In total the federal privatization programme has netted some DM 10.5 billion over nine years (£3.75 billion), a mere tenth of British privatization proceeds (£34.9 billion) between 1979 and 1988. However, the jewel in the crown of federal state enterprises is only just being prepared for privatization, namely the post office telecommunications subsidiary *Telekom*, valued at DM 50–70 billion with a turnover in 1991 of DM 47 billion. Following a protracted debate on the future of the *Bundespost* (see Humphreys, 1989), the Federal Post was split into three in 1989: the loss-making postal service and the profitable bank and telecom sections. No firm date has been fixed for the part or whole privatization of *Telekom*, though federal budget constraints will probably accelerate the process. The sale of a further share in *Lufthansa* has been postponed because of its 'poor profit position' (Economics Ministry statement, 16.7.92).

The regulatory provisions for privatized companies have not altered in Germany as they have in Britain with the sale of the monopoly utilities. The sale of *Telekom* will require some statutory controls, even if the effective telephone monopoly is modified, given the economy of scale advantages that *Telekom* has established with its ongoing programme of investments. The postal service, bereft of the internal cross-subsidy from telecom profits, is obliged by the 1989 law to rationalize and achieve profitability, even though privatization is not envisaged. There has, however, been discussion about the part-privatization of the heavily subsidised Federal Railways as part of a radical review of transport policies (*Frankfurter Rundschau*, 9.5.92).

The privatization programme adopted in 1983 should clearly be distinguished from the process of privatization going on in Eastern Germany, which cannot be dealt with in full here. However, there are important common features that should be noted. The privatized enterprises in the East will, with very few exceptions, be subject to the same re-regulated conditions as now apply in the West. The programme of privatization by the *Treuhandanstalt* is proceeding under the banner of de-concentration and the spreading of productive wealth, whereby employee share schemes have been encouraged. On the broader front, privatization in the East can arguably be seen as an icebreaker for increased deregulation, particularly in the area of broadcasting, telecommunications, health care and labour markets (Priewe and Hickel, 1991). Housing problems in the East, on the other hand, can be seen to have contributed to the reversal of the State's attempt to withdraw from responsibility and introduce greater competition.

## CONCLUSION: A ROUGHER ROAD WITH FEWER SIGNPOSTS

The results of the deregulation programme and of supply-sidism in general are a matter of considerable controversy. While it is clearly possible to assess the net benefits/net disadvantages of deregulation in specific areas (retailing, housing, financial services), the universal appeal of the programme and the need for brevity make it more appropriate here to assess the degree to which the 'manifesto' of German deregulators has been realized against the backdrop of international deregulation.

Flexible exchange rates, as advocated by Friedmann and others for years (Friedmann, 1953) have palpably failed to achieve the expected world market equilibrium for commodities and capital. World economic growth rates have maintained a downward trend, long-term real interest rates have risen sharply over the period, structural unemployment is now firmly bedded in most OECD countries, the balance of world trade is more extreme with high structural surpluses and high structural deficits in individual countries and finally the global distribution of wealth has become more grimly inequitable. To ascribe all these negative developments solely to deregulated exchange rates would be absurd, but there is an increasing consensus that they are a major contributory factor and that the experiment has failed appallingly (Strange, 1988; Herr and Voy, 1989); hence the attempts by the G7 countries and the EC to reregulate currency markets. In a broader sense this global deregulation gave a massive push to the increasing global nature of production and distribution and more specifically to the competition between states to create the most attractive location for both financial and real investment (*Standortwettbewerb*).

The global failure of currency deregulation is thus the backdrop for the national deregulation programmes that developed through the 1980s. The compulsion to adjust was as much a feature of German policies as the confident vision of *Wende* policies. In one sense it is unfair to assess the results of the programme as early as 1992, since the job is only half done: the 97 detailed proposals of the Deregulation Commission and the government's newly published privatization plans confirm this: nevertheless, notwithstanding the significance of 1992, there is sufficient evidence to allow a tentative interim audit of *Wende* politics, using predicted results as yardsticks.

Arguably one chief aim of supply-sidism – to produce cost efficiencies in production and the delivery of services – has been achieved, inasmuch as since 1982 gross wages have grown more slowly than national income, and labour productivity has risen faster than GDP (Goldberg, 1988); the accumulated labour cost saving between 1979 and 1989 has been calculated at some DM 75 billion (AAW, 1990). The negative trend of capital productivity and the net rate of profit from 1960 to 1980 was reversed in the 1980s. Against this has to be set the continuing decline in the growth rates of GDP and labour productivity, the sectoral differences between the productivity advances of manufacturing and the weaker productivity growth of the expanding service sector, and the continued but slower substitution of labour by capital (Müller, 1990), bringing with it dangers of overcapacity. Furthermore, Germany's performance has been only average by EC standards, below average if one discounts the distorting effect of the unification boom.

Most importantly, the expected multiplicator effects of cost-relief developments have not materialized. While the *profits ratio* rose by 6 percentage points between 1980 and 1988, the *investments ratio* (gross investments as a proportion of GNP) declined from 23.9 per cent to 20.9 per cent and *employment growth* was negative in the same period, averaging −0.1 per cent p.a. Notwithstanding time-lags, this key element of supply-side deregulatory politics would seem to have been a failure in Germany. An obvious reason for this apparent failure is the fact that deregulation is an international agenda, pursued with equal fervour by other nations, eager to create optimal conditions for inward investment and the valorization of 'national capital'. This 'location-competition' between nations would only make sense if it were matched by corresponding increases in real global competition and a deconcentration of capital. The opposite is true, however, making 'location-competition' a zero sum game.

Horizontal *concentration ratios* – the proportion of branch production by the top ten firms – have increased in Germany (AAW, 1988). There has been some deconcentration in terms of employment, such that small and medium-sized firms have increased their share of the employed population (Sengenberger, 1988), but this is widely interpreted as a result of differentiated employment and production strategies on the part of large companies (Semlinger, 1989; Sengenberger, 1988), contract-labour, sub-contracted production being employed to reduce the direct and marginal wage costs of the core labour force. Likewise there is no evidence of marked deconcentration from either stock market reforms or the privatization programme. While some small shareholdings have been increasingly used to advance a variety of causes in company AGMs, most small portfolios are mopped up by the bank-led proxy system. The privatization of *VEBA*, the energy conglomerate, saw a strengthening of direct bank holdings and indirect proxy control (AAW, 1990).

The 'roll-back' of the State was partly achieved in the reduction of the *State ratio* (expenditure of area authorities to GNP) from 33 per cent in 1979 to 31 per cent in 1989, but largely as a result of cutbacks in State investment from 11.5 per cent of State expenditure down to 8.8 per cent (1964: 17.8 per cent!); however, the expected fiscal consolidation has also not materialized; the *State debt ratio* rose from 30 to 41 per cent in the same period, essentially to fund tax cuts and stimulate private investment.

The key theoretical assertions concerning deregulation and privatization, that they a) would create higher profits, higher investment and increased employment and b) through a lower State ratio would produce a 'crowding-in' of private investment cannot be validated from the evidence of practice in Germany. The distribution of income is more inequitable, with logical consequences for wealth distribution, for consumer demand and, with the decline of State investment demand, for aggregate demand. Proponents of deregulation argue that the poor performance of the 1980s is the result of insufficient reductions of the 'web of pervasive market regulations' in Germany (OECD, 1988), particularly in labour market conditions (OECD, 1990b). What they ignore are the instabilities and the asymmetries that international and national programmes of deregulation have already created, above all the strengthening of the structural power of private capital and the weakening of the power of the State and of labour as factors not just of supply but of demand and hence market equilibrium. The worldwide decline in wage ratios means a relative decline in global consumer demand, the worldwide campaign for reduced State ratios implies a relative reduction in collective investment demand. Why should global enterprises invest in increased capacity when the prospects for global demand for their goods and services are less rosy? Far better to take refuge in defensive mergers or in the seductive delights of capital market speculation than to tie up reserves in unwanted capacity.

While there is obviously scope for weeding out bureaucratic hindrances to efficiency (e.g. in insurance, in energy production and supply and in construction) the case for radical deregulation in Germany remains unproven and, in many ways, dangerously naive. The case for more and better regulations in the area of capital markets, competition and the environment and at both the national and global level remains far more persuasive (Strange, 1988: 11; AAW, 1990: 158).

## NOTE

1 For a discussion of the other major area of market-led deregulation in Germany, namely that of telecommunications, see Humphreys (1992) and Woolcock (1991).

## BIBLIOGRAPHY

Adamy, W. (1988) Deregulieurung des Arbeitsmarktes – Zwischenbilanz des Beschäftigungs-förderungsgesetzes, *WSI-Mitteilungen*, 8/88.

Altvater, E. (1992) *Die Zukunft des Marktes*. Verlag Westfälisches Dampfboot, Münster.

Arbeitsgruppe Alternative Wirtschaftspolitik (1988) Wirtschaftsmacht in der Marktwirtschaft. Zur ökonomischen Konzentration in der Bundesrepublik. Cologne, Pahl-Rugenstein.

Arbeitsgruppe Alternative Wirtschaftspolitik (1989) *Memorandum '89*. Cologne, Pahl-Rugenstein.

Arbeitsgruppe Alternative Wirtschaftspolitik (1991) *Memorandum '91*. Cologne, Papyrossa.

Besters, H. (1990) Hindernisse für Vollbeschäftigung, *aus politik und zeitgeschichte*, B/18.

Biedenkopf, K. and Miegel, M. (1979) *Die programmierte Krise*. Bonn, Bonn-Aktuell.

Bosch, G. (1988) Der bundesdeutsche Arbeitsmarkt im internationalen Vergleich: 'Eurosklerose' oder 'Modell Deutschland'?, *WSI-Mitteilungen*, 3/88.

Bulmer, S. and Humphreys, P. (1989) Kohl, corporatism and congruence: the West German model under challenge. In S. Bulmer (ed.) *The Changing Agenda of West German Public Policy*. Aldershot, Dartmouth.

Bulmer, S. (ed.) (1989a) *The Changing Agenda of West German Public Policy*. Aldershot, Dartmouth.

Bundesministerium für Finanzen (1987) *Finanzbericht 1987*. Bonn.

Christlich-Demokratische Union (CDU) (1984a) *Deutschlands Zukunft als moderne und humane Industrienation. Stuttgarter Leitsätze für die 80er Jahre*. Bonn.

Christlich-Demokratische Union (1984b) *Erneuerung des Sozialen Marktwirtschaft. Materialien zur Diskussion der Stuttgarter Leitsätze*. Bonn.

Däubler, W. (1988) Deregulierung und Flexibilisierung im Arbeitsrecht, *WSI-Mitteilungen*, 8/88.

Deregulierungskommission (1991) *Marktöffnung und Wettbewerb*. Stuttgart, Poeschel.

Dombois, R. (1989) Flexibility by law? The West German Employment Protection Act and temporary employment. *Cambridge Journal of Economics*, Vol. 13.

Dyson, K. (1986) State, banks and industry: the West German case. In A. Cox (ed.) *State, Finance and Industry*. Brighton, Wheatsheaf.

European Commission (EC) (1988) *The 'Cost of Non-Europe' in Financial Services; Research on the 'Cost of Non-Europe', Basic Findings*, Vol. 9. Luxemburg.

Fehr, E. (1990) Die Auswirkungen der Gewerkschaften auf die Allokationseffizienz im Lichte einiger Besonderheiten des Arbeitsmarktes, *WSI-Mitteilungen*, 6/90.

Friedmann, M. (1953) The case for flexible exchange rates. In *Essays in Positive Economics*. Chicago, Chicago University Press.

Glastetter, W., Paulert, R. and Spörel, U. (1983) *Die wirtschaftliche Entwicklung in der Bundesrepublik Deutschland 1950–1980*. Frankfurt, Campus.

Goldberg, J. (1988) *Von Krise zu Krise. Die Wirtschaft der Bundesrepublik im Umbruch*. Cologne, Pahl-Rugenstein.

Herr, H.-J. and Voy, K. (1989) *Währungskonkurrenz und Deregulierung der Weltwirtschaft*. Marburg, Metropolis.

Hickel, R. (1991) Befreite Arbeitsmärkte. Zum Endbericht der 'Deregulierungs-kommission', *Blätter für deutsche und internationale Politik*, 6/91.

Humphreys, P. (1989) Policies for technological innovation and industrial change. In S. Bulmer (ed.) *The Changing Agenda of West German Public Policy*. Aldershot, Dartmouth.

Humphreys, P. (1992) 'The European Community and pan-European broadcasting'. *Journal of Area Studies*, New series 1.

Institut der deutschen Wirtschaft (IW) (1988) *Standort Bundesrepublik Deutschland*. *iw-trends*, 2/88.

Kartte, W. (1992) Wir sind doch nicht blind. Interview in *Der Spiegel*, 15/1992.

Keller, B. (1989) Ein Irrweg der Deregulieuring: Das Beschäftigungsförderungs-gesetz, *WSI-Mitteilungen*, 5/89.

Keller, B. (1990) Noch mehr De-Regulierung oder stärkere Re-Regulierung?, *WSI-Mitteilungen*, 6/90.

Kennedy, E. (1991) *The Bundesbank. Germany's Central Bank in the International Monetary System*. London, Pinter.

Keuchel, M. (1989) *Kann der Arbeitsmarkt dem Wettbewerb unterworfen werden?*. Cologne, University of Cologne Institute of Economic Policy.

Küchle, H. (1990) Kündigungsschutzvorschriften im europäischen Vergleich, *WSI-Mitteilungen*, 6/90.

Leaman, J. (1988) *The Political Economy of West Germany – An Introduction*. London, Macmillan.

Leaman, J. (1991) The paradox of West Germany's political economy in a period of critical readjustment. In A.M. Brassloff and W. Brassloff (eds) *European Insights*. Amsterdam, Elsevier.

Lijphart, A. and Crepaz, M. (1991) Corporatism and consensus democracy in eighteen countries. Conceptual and empirical linkages, *British Journal of Political Science*, April, Vol. 22/2.

Merklein, R. (1985) Die Sklerose der deutschen Wirtschaft. *Der Spiegel*, 1/1985.

Möller, C. (1988) Flexibilisierung – Eine Talfahrt in die Armut – Prekäre Arbeits-verhältnisse im Dienstleistungssektor, *WSI-Mitteilungen*, 8/88.

Monopolkommission (1988) *Die Wettbewerbsordnung erweitern. Hauptgutachten 1986/87*. Baden-Baden, Nomos.

Moran, M. (1989) A state of inaction: the state and stock exchange reform in the Federal Republic of Germany. In S. Bulmer (ed.) *The Changing Agenda of West German Public Policy*. Aldershot, Dartmouth.

Moran, M. (1992) Regulatory change in German financial markets. In K. Dyson (ed.) *The Politics of German Regulation*. Aldershot, Gower.

Müller, G. (1990) Makroökonomische Faktoren der Anpassungsfähigkeit des

Arbeitsmarktes der Bundesrepublik Deutschland, *WSI-Mitteilungen*, 6/90.

Müller, G. and Seifert, H. (1990) Zur Bedeutung von Regulierungen auf dem Arbeitsmarkt, *WSI-Mitteilungen*, 6/90.

Müller, G. and Seifert, H. (1991) Deregulierung aus Prinzip? Eine Diskussion der Vorschläge der Deregulierungskommission zum Arbeitsmarkt, *WSI-Mitteilungen*, 8/91.

Noll, Roger G. and Owen, Bruce M. (1983) *The Political Economy of Deregulation. Interest Groups in the Regulatory Process*. Washington and London, AE Institute.

OECD (1988) *OECD Economic Surveys. Germany 1987/1988*. Paris.

OECD (1990a) *OECD Economic Surveys. Germany 1989/1990*. Paris.

OECD (1990b) *Progress in Structural Reform*. Paris.

Pfeiffer, H. (1989) *Die Macht am Main*. Cologne, Pahl-Rugenstein.

Priewe, J. and Hickel, R. (1991) *Der Preis der Einheit*. Frankfurt am Main, Fischer.

Riege, M. (1989) Aufhebung der Wohnungsgemeinnützigkeit – Die Deregulierung des Wohnungsmarktes schreitet voran, *WSI-Mitteilungen*, 9/89.

Semlinger, K. (1989) Fremdleistungsbezug als Flexibilitätsreservoir, *WSI-Mitteilungen*, 9/89.

Sengenberger, W. (1988) Mehr Beschäftigung in Klein- und Mittelbetrieben: Ein Flexibilitätsgewinn, *WSI-Mitteilungen*, 8/88.

Stimpel, R., Canibol, H.-P. and Fuchs, H. (1992) Bürokratischer Irrsinn. Wohnungsbau in Deutschland ist teuer . . ., *WirtschaftsWoche*, 31.1.1992.

Strange, S. (1986) *Casino Capitalism*. Oxford, Blackwell.

Strange, S. (1988) *States and Markets*. London, Pinter.

Swann, D. (1992) Standards, procurement, mergers and state aids. In D. Swann (ed.) *The Single European Market and Beyond*. London, Routledge.

Wolf, V. (1992) Schlechte Karten, *WirtschaftsWoche*, 8.5.1992.

Wolowicz, E. (1990) Zwischen Staatsintervention und freiem Spiel. Entwicklung der Wohnungsbau- und Mietrechtpolitik in der Bundesrepublik Deutschland. In C. Ude (ed.) *Wege aus der Wohnungsnot*. Munich, Piper.

Woolcock, S., Hodges, M. and Schreiber, K. (1991) *Britain, Germany and 1992. The Limits of Deregulation*. London, Pinter.

Zachert, U. (1988) Entwicklung und Perspektiven des Normalarbeitsverhältnisses, *WSI-Mitteilungen*, 8/88.

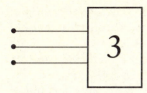

# PRIVATIZATION AND REGULATORY CHANGE: THE CASE OF GREAT BRITAIN

## Tony Prosser and Michael Moran

One of the best descriptions of the early economic policies of the Thatcher governments is entitled *Mrs Thatcher's Economic Experiment* (Keegan, 1984). This suggests an important truth about the British privatization programme; it can be seen as a large-scale economic experiment, a testing of a set of economic ideals. This is not to say that it was inspired by a single, clear ideological rationale; it was the result of a shifting mix of motives in which the poor performance of public enterprises, the cutting of public borrowing, the destruction of political constituencies hostile to the Conservative Party and increasing share-ownership all played a part (Heald and Steel, 1982; Graham and Prosser, 1991: 8–13, 19–28). Nevertheless, although many earlier individual examples of privatization existed in other countries, the implementation of such a large-scale programme was quite new in British economic management and, as the events described in this book witness, its success has inspired world-wide imitation.

In this chapter, however, we wish to stress the peculiarities of the United Kingdom constitutional, political and financial systems that made implementation of such a programme possible, but that at the same time make it difficult simply to transfer the British model to other nations. Within the economic case for privatization, little attention has been paid to the importance of national characteristics shaping implementation; property rights and markets have been assumed to be much the same throughout the capitalist or incipiently capitalist world. Yet experience has already shown that these national characteristics are of crucial importance in the project of moving to a market economy. In particular, systems of property rights and functioning markets do not simply create themselves when the State withdraws; both have to be painfully constructed by public and private actors; the political programmes to achieve these changes can easily be derailed, especially in conditions where democracy is a young and fragile flower. In Britain, by contrast, not only were the financial preconditions of a market economy particularly well developed, but a government with a majority in the House of Commons is able to implement policy with a minimum of constitutional constraint. As a result, the 'economic experiment', could probably not have taken place in any other Western economy. Before examining the reasons for this it will be useful to outline the scale of the British programme.

## THE BRITISH PRIVATIZATION PROGRAMME

Although it is important not to neglect the pragmatic political influences on privatization, which did much to shape its development, privatization in Britain appeared to be a more consistent and planned programme than that in other nations. Thus after limited beginnings it became based around ambitious targets for the raising of revenue each year, targets that, unlike in the case of, say, Italy, were met. The Government succeeded in selling off all but four of the major public enterprises; the exceptions (British Coal, British Rail, London Regional Transport and the Post Office) face total or partial privatization during the current (1992–7) Parliament. In 1991 the target receipts were £8 billion for 1991–2 and 1992–3, and £5.5 billion for the two following financial years. Table 3.1 gives the proceeds of privatization and relates them to overall government expenditure and Table 3.2 lists up to the end of 1991 the major Stock Market flotations by which the largest enterprises have been sold.

Nor did this represent the whole of the privatization programme; a large number of private sales took place, either by government selling smaller enterprises or by enterprises themselves disposing of subsidiaries, normally after governmental pressure to do so. By early 1990 such sales had raised over £2,500,000 (for a list see Graham and Prosser, 1991: 106–7), and they included many of the most controversial examples of privatization, for example the sale of the Rover Group carmaker and the armaments firm Royal Ordnance, both to the already privatized British Aerospace.

Even in the case of the private sales, then, privatization was essentially government-directed and did not involve enterprises themselves taking strategic commercial decisions. How was government able to undertake such a programme so quickly and with few apparent setbacks? The answer lies

**Table 3.1**   UK privatization proceeds

| Privatization receipts | | Planning total | Central govt. expenditure |
| --- | --- | --- | --- |
| 1979–80 | 377 | 77,600 | 52,700 |
| 1980–81 | 210 | 92,700 | 64,100 |
| 1981–82 | 493 | 104,000 | 73,800 |
| 1982–83 | 455 | 113,600 | 82,400 |
| 1983–84 | 1,139 | 120,400 | 86,200 |
| 1984–85 | 2,050 | 130,000 | 93,200 |
| 1985–86 | 2,707 | 133,700 | 99,600 |
| 1986–87 | 4,460 | 139,300 | 106,100 |
| 1987–88 | 5,140 | 145,800 | 111,200 |
| 1988–89 | 7,073 | 149,600 | 116,300 |
| 1989–90 | 4,200 | 162,900 | 127,500 |
| 1990–91 | 5,300 | 180,000 | 140,600 |
| 1991–92 | 7,900 | 204,700 | 156,600 |

*Source*: Government Expenditure Plans, 1989–90 to 1992–3, Cm 1021; Financial Statement and Budget Report 1992–3, HC 319. All figures are in £ million; those for 1991–2 are estimated outturns.

*Note*: Figures for privatization receipts represent net receipts, but it should be noted that they are an underestimate of the proceeds from the entire programme as they exclude receipts from private sales paid to the industries themselves but then compensated for by adjustment of the industries' borrowing requirements. The planning total represents all public expenditure, including that by local authorities and the external finance requirements of public corporations.

partly in the absence of political and legal constraints on a British government wishing to implement such a policy, and partly in the highly-developed nature of British financial institutions. We shall begin by describing some of the sources of legal controversy in privatizations elsewhere, and explain how they were either non-existent or easily resolved in Britain.

*The unitary State*

The first peculiarity of the United Kingdom that has simplified the privatization process is the unitary structure of the nation; this leaves no entrenched spheres of jurisdiction for state or local government, and so the process has not been hindered by problems of the division of property rights or of competence to privatize between different geographical levels of government. Nor has it been hindered by the existence of public enterprises at State level beyond the legal control of central government. The obvious contrast is with the republics of the former Soviet Union; moreover, even before the elections of 1992 hastened a split in Czechoslovakia, an OECD report on the implementation of marketization in that nation had highlighted the major

**Table 3.2**   The main UK privatizations

| Company | Gross proceeds (£ million) |
| --- | --- |
| British Petroleum (1979) | 290.4 |
| British Aerospace (1981) | 148.6 |
| Cable and Wireless (1981) | 223.9 |
| Amersham International (1982) | 71.0 |
| Britoil (1982) | 548.8 |
| Associated British Ports (1983) | 52.4 |
| British Petroleum (1983) | 565.5 |
| Cable and Wireless (1983) | 275.0 |
| Associated British Ports (1984) | 52.4 |
| Enterprise Oil (1984) | 392.2 |
| Jaguar (1984) | 293.5 |
| British Telecom (1984) | 3915.6 |
| British Aerospace (1985) | 550.7 |
| Britoil (1985) | 448.8 |
| Cable and Wireless (1985) | 932.9 |
| British Gas (1986) | 5434.4 |
| British Airways (1987) | 900.3 |
| Rolls Royce (1987) | 1362.5 |
| British Airports Authority (1987) | 1281.3 |
| British Petroleum (1987) | 5727.0 |
| British Steel Corporation (1988) | 2482.0 |
| Water Authorities (1989) | 5240.0 |
| Electricity Distribution Companies (1990) | 5200.0 |
| Electricity Generation Companies (1991) | 2200.0 |
| Scottish Electricity Companies (1991) | 2900.0 |
| British Telecom (1991) | 5350.0 |

*Source*: Graham and Prosser, 1991.

problem as being the lack of a clear resolution of the roles of the Czech and Slovak Republics (*Financial Times*, 8 January 1992). Even in the pre-unification Federal Republic of Germany the process of privatization was slowed by the fact that market holdings in the energy and financial sectors were at State rather than at federal level (Esser, 1988).

By contrast, in Britain the centralization of power in Whitehall simply prevents these problems from impeding government in implementing ambitious privatization policies. Indeed, the earliest major privatization initiative involved central government compelling local government to sell council houses, and by the 1987 election over a million homes had been sold. In the absence of any entrenched field of competence for local government the latter is powerless to resist legislation from the centre imposing such policies. There are two exceptions to the geographical unity of the privatization programme; the privatization of the Scottish electricity industry in vertically integrated form, unlike its counterparts south of the border, and the retention of water supply (perhaps temporarily) in the hands of Scottish regional authorities. However, the reasons for these exceptions were technical and historical; neither was based on any constitutional problems limiting the powers of government to impose privatization on Scotland.

## Property rights

The question of definition and allocation of property rights in enterprises being privatized has arisen in acute form in Central and Eastern Europe. Apart from the initial problem of establishing a workable system of such rights, the question of the rights of the original, pre-nationalization owners of the enterprises, involving land and also some industrial concerns, has seriously delayed some aspects of privatization. Thus, most strikingly, this problem of restitution has been the subject of decisions by the Hungarian Constitutional Court, as described by Pogany in Chapter 8.

In Britain there are no entrenched rights to property. The European Convention on Human Rights imposes certain constraints on the taking of property, but in a case involving Britain it was made clear that the margin of appreciation allowed a government wishing to nationalize is so great that no British nationalization would have breached it (*Lithgow v. United Kingdom* [1986] 8 EHRR 329). The question of the rights of the original owners of nationalized property will therefore not arise. Two cases did reach the British courts concerned with the legal basis for the ownership of enterprises being privatized. The first, *Ross v. Lord Advocate* [1986] WLR 1077, reached the House of Lords, the highest court in the British legal system, and concerned the rights of depositors in relation to the surplus assets of the Trustee Savings Bank, then being sold. However, it was a highly technical case dealing with no important issues of principle. Similarly, in *Sheffield City Council v. Yorkshire Water Services Ltd* [1991] 2 All ER 290, the Vice-Chancellor held that local authorities had no rights in the assets previously transferred from them without compensation to the water authorities, which were later privatized.

What has occurred in the case of the major British sales has been that a statute has been passed converting public corporations into limited liability companies with all shares vested in the Secretary of State, who then simply sells the shares and retains the proceeds. In the absence of entrenched rights in the British constitution the highest form of law is statute (subject to European Community law), and the concept of parliamentary sovereignty prevents the courts from reviewing the content of statutes; the courts are limited to interpreting Acts of Parliament and cannot strike them down as unconstitutional. Given the almost total control of the legislative process by a government with a majority in the House of Commons, policy can be turned into unchallengeable forms of law with little difficulty.

## A SINGLE MODEL OF PRIVATIZATION

In a number of other countries, both in Europe and elsewhere, certain enterprises have a special constitutional status making privatization more difficult. This will normally occur through their designation as public services or monopolies. Thus in France the Preamble to the 1946 Constitution, incorporated by reference into that of the Fifth Republic, provides that enterprises that have the character of a national public service or of a monopoly are to become public property, and this has been held in principle enforceable by the Conseil Constitutionnel (in effect, the French constitutional court), in reviewing privatization legislation (*decision 86–207*, 25–6 June, 1986). In Germany, the post, telecommunications and rail services are given a special constitutional status inconsistent with their privatization, and this was sufficient to force the federal government to abandon, it now seems temporarily, plans for the sale of the telecommunications enterprise after unification. Similarly, the conversion of the railways into a shareholding company will require a constitutional amendment. This will not, of course, prevent the privatization of a large number of other enterprises, and moreover a constitutional amendment for the privatization of the German air traffic control system has been approved and similar amendments in the other cases now seem likely. Nevertheless, the point remains that privatization of these enterprises cannot be treated as simply an ordinary example of government policy; the constitution imposes special constraints, the overcoming of which can impose extra political costs. For example, the Social Democratic Party was able to make its necessary support for such an amendment in the case of the telecommunications business conditional on wide-ranging guarantees for the workforce and the retention of a State monopoly of terrestrial telephone networks. This is in marked contrast to the negligible influence of the Parliamentary opposition in the British privatization programme.

For the reasons set out in the previous section, parliamentary sovereignty in Britain enables any enterprise to be privatized in the same way, and a similar procedure has been adopted for the utilities such as the electricity companies and enterprises in competitive markets such as British Steel. The only legal challenge to the scope of a disposal was a case brought by the Port of London Police Federation seeking leave for judicial review of the privatization of port police as part of the sale of Tilbury Docks under the Ports Act 1991. The Federation argued that express authorization was needed in the statute for the transfer of police functions to a private company, a proposition roundly rejected by the High Court in refusing leave to bring the action: 'I am unable to hold that it is arguable that, given the nature of police functions, specific provision was required on constitutional or any other grounds for the transfer of the police force.' (Pill LJ in *R. v. Secretary of State for Transport ex parte Port of London Police Authority*, Queen's Bench Division, 17 January 1992, LEXIS). In practice, a standard set of provisions has been developed for inclusion in each privatization statute, although these merely provide a framework enabling the transfer of property rights and the sale of shares, detailed issues of institutional design and relations with government being dealt with in the articles of association of the new company. The major difference between the utilities and the enterprises operating in competitive markets is that regulatory controls are needed in the former case, and these will be described below.


## VALUATION

The next peculiarity of British experience concerns the valuation of enterprises as part of the privatization process. Once more, the degree of freedom available to the British government is striking. In brief, the issue of valuation has been treated as no different from that in a sale by a private owner, and no particular protection for any public interest has been imposed in the process, although it may be examined after the sale by the National Audit Office and the Public Accounts Committee of the House of Commons. Thus the minister will take advice from a merchant bank in valuing the company, though it is purely up to him to decide on the eventual share price. Up to the British Steel sale in 1988, the bank advising him was also an underwriter for the sale, thus committing itself to buy unsold shares for a fixed commission and therefore creating a conflict of interests. Again the contrast with France is striking, for there the Conseil Constitutionnel held that it would be unconstitutional to sell public enterprises at an unduly low price *inter alia* because allowing purchasers of shares to profit at public expense would breach the right to equality between citizens. As a result, the government was forced to establish the Privatization Commission as an independent source of valuation for enterprises being sold, and the minister was not allowed to set prices at below the level suggested by the Commission's valuation.

In the more recent flotations the British government has adopted more sophisticated techniques involving partial tenders and the sale of only part of its holding at once. Nevertheless, there has been extensive criticism of underpricing in the privatization process. This has laid the government open to the charge that public assets are being sold on the cheap; less obviously, it may also have limited the achievement of its objective of wider share ownership. At first sight impressive results seem to have been achieved, with the number of individuals owning shares increasing from 3 million to 10 million since 1979. However, the proportion of shares owned by private individuals has actually *declined* during the privatization programme. This has occurred partly because it is rational for an investor to sell his or her shares as soon after dealings begin as possible in order to take advantage of the high initial premiums; the purchasers will be the large institutions whose direct allocation of shares was limited to permit participation by small investors. The result is that purchase of shares in privatized concerns does not offer any real introduction to the experience of normal share ownership but rather gives the appearance of a gamble with an almost guaranteed win. Nor do the initial premiums give an accurate picture as to the subsequent performance of the shares; whereas shares in the utilities have generally outperformed the market, those in enterprises in competitive markets such as British Steel are now often at a level below their original offer price.

Serious accusations of underpricing have also been made in relation to the private sales, to a large extent based on allegations that the government did not properly assess the development value of land transferred in the sales. Thus Royal Ordnance, the major manufacturer of armaments and ammunition for the army, was sold to the already privatized British Aerospace for £190 million; this included some sites likely to be suitable for development which were valued at £13.6 million. A later report suggested that their development value was no less than £462 million; the Public Accounts Committee, while considering this estimate to be too high, estimated their value at considerably more than that reflected in the sale price and proposed that provision for a clawback of part of future development profits to the Treasury be included in future sales (HC 448, 1988–9). Such a provision was adopted in the sale of the water authorities, but more recently the Committee has criticized the failure to claw back large development profits on bus station sites after the sale of the subsidiaries of the National Bus Company (HC 119, 1990–1).

A further controversial issue of underpricing concerns the large cash injections and writing-off of debts which have accompanied some private sales. It has appeared that the government has been so eager to accomplish privatization that it has agreed to sale on almost any terms, and in a number of cases the receipts it has received have been negative after taking into account the financial contributions made to ensure a sale. The most celebrated example is the sale of the Rover Group, the last remaining large-scale British car manufacturer, to British Aerospace, which was granted exclusive negotiating rights. The original deal concluded was that BAe would pay a price of £150 million, while the government would inject £800 million into the business to wipe out debts. However, the European Commission insisted that this be reduced to £469 million plus £78 million regional assistance. It later became apparent that the government had made secret concessions not notified to the Commission to ensure that the deal still took place, and British Aerospace is now being required to pay back the additional payments. As the Public Accounts Committee observed, 'British Aerospace acquired owner-ship of Rover at such a price as to enable it to cover most of the purchase price by disposal of a few of its assets' (HC 34 1990–1, para. 24).

The story of the latter sale demonstrates an important theme, to which we shall return at the conclusion of this book, the European Commission now plays an important role in relation to privatization decision-making. In this case its concern was to police State aids to avoid distortion of fair competition within the Community; and it should be stressed that privatization is not automatically a force for increasing competition. Indeed, one of the pervasive themes in British privatization has been that, during the privatization process, both the enterprises being disposed of and the potential purchasers will seek to obtain special competitive advantages for the enterprise as part of the deal; the temptation for government will be to grant these to enable privatization to take place easily even if at the expense of open markets. This is a theme that has occurred also in relation to the large flotations of shares where the temptation is to limit competition and regulation in order to make the sales possible and to increase the proceeds for government by means of a higher share price (for the seminal statement of this theme see Kay and Silberstrom, 1984). We shall return to the problems created when we discuss regulation later in this chapter; the relevance of the tension beween privatization and competition is of obvious importance for Eastern and Central Europe, where competition policy is in its infancy.

## FINANCIAL MARKETS

To readers concerned with privatization in Eastern and Central Europe, these concerns about pricing might seem of limited importance; rather than getting prices right, the concern will be to establish any reliable system of pricing. Of course, the role of the financial markets will be crucial here, and once more we find that the British experience displays important differences from that experienced elsewhere. The newly marketizing economies of Eastern Europe, of course, have to construct a financial system virtually from the foundations. Any ambitious system of privatization will place extreme demands on financial institutions. The key factor to bear in mind in the British case is that the financial system is uniquely equipped to service the sort of large-scale privatization programme pursued by British governments in recent years; and it must also be borne in mind that the financial system in Britain is unusual even by the standards of advanced capitalist countries, and that its unusual features are the product of particular characteristics of British historical development and are therefore unlikely to be replicated elsewhere.

Britain was a pioneer of industrialization; at the same time her imperial history and her position as a trading nation made the financial and trading interests of the City of London especially important. The result is that in the latter half of the twentieth century the country is marked by two unique features: there has been a historical separation between many of the most important financial markets, such as the Stock Exchange, and the industrial manufacturing sector; and London has remained a major centre of international banking, despite the relative decline of the remainder of the British economy. As a leading world financial centre London is endowed with an ideal institutional apparatus for large-scale stock flotations. Selling public enterprises obviously demands a supply of buyers, but it also demands a wide range of specialized services: lawyers to determine contracts, individuals or institutions willing to underwrite share issues, market makers prepared to ensure that stock, once bought, can be traded on. In London there is a concentration of commercial legal skill, underwriting facilities and market making resources unmatched anywhere outside the United States. The British financial system, therefore, facilitated privatization because it supplied the services necessary for privatization on a large scale to take place. But it was also one of the sources of the demand for privatization. The vast volume of business in commercial services like underwriting and issue management generated by the flotations was a considerable incentive to the City to support the privatization programme. Nor was the domestic privatization programme the only incentive: the experience built up in the flotations at home helped City institutions to establish a world lead as consultants in foreign privatizations.

Thus the financial system in Britain has, as far as privatization programmes are concerned, a double uniqueness: even by the standards of other capitalist nations, such as Italy, the Stock Market is uniquely highly developed; while the financial markets in the City of London have a uniquely important place in the world financial system. Any attempt to emulate the British privatization programme has to bear in mind that the financial features central to the programme cannot be replicated elsewhere, least of all in economic systems just emerging from the grip of command economies.

## REGULATION: CAPITAL MARKETS

We have suggested earlier that privatization and competition may be in tension; for privatization to be successful as part of the process of market building it is necessary that there be developed competition law and policy and regulatory structures to deal with those enterprises where competition cannot be introduced. In both these respects we find once more that Britain has marked advantages over other nations.

Apart from that of Germany, British competition law and policy is the best developed in the European Community. Just as important is the fact that its form offers especial advantages to government. Especially when compared with anti-trust policies in the United States, it is characterized by the broad discretion given to government and the very limited role played by individuals; 'the structure of our anti-trust legislation vividly demonstrates the retention of ultimate control by the political arm of government' (Craig, 1987: 217). The system is thus dominated by bargaining, largely in secret and unregulated by any public law mechanisms (for an outline of those aspects of competition law relevant to privatization, see Graham and Prosser, 1991: 199–203). This enables the government to have the best of both worlds; on the one hand there is a developed system of competition policy that can be used to create and maintain open markets where necessary, but on the other hand it remains firmly under governmental control and so can be prevented from coming to decisions that undermine other governmental policies such as the privatization programme. For example, when Royal Ordnance was sold to British Aerospace there were a number of complaints to the Office of Fair Trading from other defence contractors that this would inhibit competition in key areas of military procurement. However, in a merger case the decision to refer to the Monopolies and Mergers Commission is at the discretion of the Secretary of State. British Aerospace had made the sale conditional on non-referral to the Commission, and it was hardly surprising that the Secretary of State did not make a reference; instead assurances were received from the company that the Ministry of Defence would have the right to inspect its books to detect whether it was using Royal Ordnance as a preferred source of supplies at below market rates. It is instructive that the major intervention against a privatization deal on the grounds of its giving an unfair competitive advantage (that concerning the Rover group) came from the European Commission, not from the domestic competition authorities.

Further control over the operation of the capital markets has been afforded the government through the system of 'golden shares', complex provisions that give it a power of veto, temporary or permanent, over certain decisions of privatized enterprises; in particular power to veto unwelcome takeovers (for details, see Graham and Prosser, 1991: 141–51). Once more the exercise or non-exercise of these powers is purely at the discretion of government, and they are outside effective legal control. The only effective intervention over their exercise has come from the European Commission, which gained a partial lifting of the provisions relating to Rolls-Royce and British Aerospace after complaints from investors forced to sell shares because of restrictions on foreign holdings contained in them.

It is clear, then, that government will wish to retain some forms of control over the operation of the capital markets after privatization; the British system has permitted this through the highly discretionary nature of competition law and through the use of golden shares. Similar conclusions can be drawn from an examination of the regulation of product markets after privatization.

## REGULATION: PRODUCT MARKETS

It has already been made clear that the large public utilities have been included in the privatization programme, and it is this that distinguishes it from other nations where there have been large scale disposals of competitive enterprises. A government wishing to privatize enterprises with monopoly powers can employ three possible strategies. First, it can split the enterprise, thereby creating a new competitive market. Second, it can preserve the enterprise intact but encourage the growth of competitors, or third it can privatize the enterprise with monopoly powers retained but subject to regulatory machinery. Examples of all three approaches can be found in the British privatization programme, but in practice the third has been by far the most important as regards the utilities.

In comparison to the United States, where the question of regulation has been prominent for far longer, Britain has a distinctive regulatory style with limited use of formally legal procedures and standards, instead relying on private bargaining (see Vogel, 1986). No doubt reflecting the pragmatism of this style, there seems to be little clear rationale or principle forming a base for the regulatory arrangements adopted in Britain. In practice, two themes have been particularly noticeable in these arrangements. First, many important powers have been retained in governmental hands. The standard model adopted for the utilities is that the Secretary of State licences operators, and so is responsible for deciding on the degree of competition, a role that has assumed considerable importance in the field of telecommunications where competitors have been licensed as well as the previously nationalized operator. The initial licence issued by the Secretary of State will contain detailed conditions effectively determining the operating environment of the enterprise. In addition he will possess a number of other important powers of intervention, particularly in relation to the water and electricity industries.

Second, the enforcement of licence conditions and a number of other tasks, such as dealing with complaints and advising the Secretary of State, have been entrusted to new independent regulators, each headed by a director-general and placed outside the structure of government departments. Although familiar from the United States, these independent regulators represent something of a departure for Britain. Again, no coherent institutional design seems to have inspired their creation and it has in general been left to the regulators themselves to develop their own procedures, in marked contrast to the United States where the Administrative Procedure Act provides a structured set of procedures for the federal agencies (see Graham and Prosser, 1991; 220–31), although more recent legislation has imposed some extra procedural protection (*Competition and Service (Utilities) Act 1992*).

The most important task of the regulators is to enforce and renegotiate at intervals the formulae limiting the annual price increases by the utilities. The structure of these formulae aimed to provide a form of regulation that involved the minimum of discretionary power for the regulator and so the model adopted linked price increases to the rate of inflation by limiting them to a specified figure above or below the annual change in the retail price index (the RPI − or + X formula) (for the origins see Littlechild 1984, 1986). In practice, however, the result has been a highly discretionary system, for the formula must be renegotiated by the regulatory authority every few years and this must be based on assessing a reasonable rate of return, precisely what the inflation-linked formula sought to avoid. It seems that the formulae set originally were too generous to the utilities, and revisions since have resulted in their becoming stricter; the lesson is that the RPI-based formula is no substitute for complex discretionary regulatory decisions, but merely allows them to be made less often.

In many industries, notably gas and telecommunications, regulation has been characterized by frequent battles between regulator and regulated industry; indeed, the Chairman of British Gas has been quoted as complaining that his enterprise now faces more intervention by the public authorities than it did under nationalization. One finds once more here the employment of the characteristic British style of regulatory bargaining. For example, the procedures for licence amendment without the consent of the privatized enterprise are highly cumbersome, involving a reference to the Monopolies and Mergers Commission, and so the far simpler process of amendment by agreement with the enterprise is much more likely to be employed. This may have advantages in negotiation of consent with the regulated enterprise but does not permit the involvement of other groups such as consumers. The contrast with the United States is again striking; there regulatory procedures have been required to take a relatively participative form by constitutional requirements of due process and by the creation of a general legislative framework in the form of the Administrative Procedure Act. In Britain, the courts have not been prepared to require more than minimal protections in economic regulation: nor does regulation by independent agency fit into existing structures of ministerial responsibility, which in this context are so attenuated as to be meaningless.

Against this problem of accountability should be set, however, the fact that the regulatory bodies have made efforts to conduct their decision-making as openly as possible; indeed, far more information is now available about the privatized utilities than was available under nationalization. Nevertheless, in the absence of legal requirements of publicity, attempts by a company to prevent disclosure of information on grounds of commercial confidentiality put the regulator in an extremely difficult position, as to disclose may undermine a number of informal norms negotiated between regulator and enterprise and on which the smooth everyday process of regulation may depend.

## CONCLUSION

It is undeniable that the British privatization programme has been on a heroic scale; almost all of the industrial public sector is now in private hands, and perhaps the most striking lesson is that there is no field of activity that cannot be privatized, from armaments to public utilities. This can partly be explained by the determination of government, and it is tempting to conclude from this that the experience can be replicated by any similarly determined government elsewhere; as the minister responsible for developing much of its thrust put it, 'Britain's privatization programme sets [a] world example' (Moore, 1986).

However, we have suggested here that the British government possessed a number of key advantages that made implementation of such a heroic programme possible. The British privatization programme was accomplished so easily because of the peculiar freedom given to a government with a parliamentary majority to implement policy free from constitutional and other legal constraints, whilst the existence of a developed system of financial markets made the technical achievement of the rapid disposal of large enterprises possible. The regulatory style characteristic of Britain also permits government to create regulatory systems easily and in a form that retains the power to determine the degree of competition and the initial operating environment for the privatized utilities in its own hands.

One further point needs to be made. The system of democratic government in Britain is sufficiently firmly established to cope with the inevitable social disruption caused by privatization and the closures necessary to pave the way for it. Thus a level of unemployment unprecedented in post-war years has not been met by the degree of political disruption predicted before 1979. Similarly, the trade unions have had minimal success in fighting privatization due to a combination of factors, including sound strategic planning by government of when and how it picks disputes with them, draconian restrictions on the unions' legal powers, their own internal divisions, and strong policing of such disputes as have arisen, notably the lengthy miners' strike of 1984–5. Privatization will inevitably have the potential to create highly disruptive social conflict; it is questionable whether newly democratic regimes will be able to manage this in the way the British government has done.

In one sense, however, the stress on the peculiar nature of British constitutional and institutional arrangements and regulatory style may already be out of date, for policy-making and implementation is now increasingly taking place on a European Community-wide basis and this is rapidly replacing central elements of national style, especially in the regulatory field. It has important implications both for the scope of privatization and the construction of regulatory systems; this is a theme which we shall examine in detail in our conclusion to this book.

## BIBLIOGRAPHY

Craig, P. (1987) The Monopolies and Mergers Commission: competition and administrative rationality. In R. Baldwin and C. McCrudden (eds) *Regulation and Public Law*. London, Weidenfeld and Nicolson.

Esser, J. (1988) Symbolic privatization: the politics of privatization in West Germany, *West European Politics*, 11(4), 61–73.

Graham, C. and Prosser, T. (1991) *Privatizing Public Enterprises: Constitutions, the State and Regulation in Comparative Perspective*. Oxford, Clarendon Press.

Heald, D. and Steel, D. (1982) Privatizing public enterprises: an analysis of the Government's case, *Political Quarterly*, 53, 333–49.

Kay, J. and Silberstrom, Z. (1984) The new industrial policy: privatization and competition, *Midland Bank Review*, (Spring), 8–16.

Keegan, W. (1984) *Mrs Thatcher's Economic Experiment*. Harmondsworth, Penguin.

Littlechild, S. (1984) *Regulation of British Telecommunications Profitability*. London, Department of Industry.

Littlechild, S. (1986) *Economic Regulation of Privatized Water Authorities*. London, Department of the Environment.

Moore, J. (1986) *Britain's Privatization Programme Sets World Example*. HM Treasury Press Release 51/86, London; also published as *Privatisation in the United Kingdom*. London, Aims of Industry.

Vogel, D. (1986) *National Styles of Regulation*. London, Cornell.

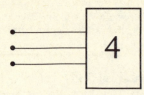

# 4

# DEREGULATION AND PRIVATIZATION IN ITALY

## Sabino Cassese

### CHARACTERISTICS OF STATE INTERVENTION IN THE ITALIAN ECONOMY

Until recently, hardly any specifically regulatory area of policy existed in Italy. There is an extensive public sector with its origins in the 1930s, though it is not the result of specific acts of nationalization of private property (the sole exception to this being that of electricity in 1962). Italy has a mixed economy, in which the use of public resources and policy instruments mingles with private economic action. Public intervention in semi-public or private areas takes place both by means of direct controls (Italy is the only industrialized country to retain a general control on prices) and through distribution of public resources (subsidies and other State aids to the private sector).

The origins of this situation are often attributed to the weakness of the market (especially during the slump of the 1930s), or else to the growing intervention of the State (accentuated during the 1960s and 1970s). However, the most important origins are to be found in the weakness of the State itself during the period of its development. The State is comprised, in essence, of its personnel. Between 1890 and 1910 a managing class had grown up within it, but fascism removed the leading administrators; instead of using the State directly it had recourse to the creation of public enterprises. However, these enterprises, intended to be the means of saving the State, in fact undermined it, themselves subjecting it to many forms of pressure.

## DEREGULATION

From this starting point, we can appreciate why deregulation has played a lesser role than has privatization. As regards the former, three tendencies can be detected. The first is the creation of exceptions to the scope of public monopolies. For example, a law passed in 1991 permitted private concerns to produce, transmit and to sell electricity. In practice, and now by law under a statute of 1990, private enterprise has also played a major part in broad-casting. However, such increases in the scope of the private sector are not associated with the relinquishing of the State's claim of basic responsibility for a sector, but only reduce the areas that it runs directly. Neverthe-less, these changes diminish the segregation between public and private sectors.

The second tendency is exemplified by the introduction in 1990 of a com-petition law. It is true that Article 8 of this law, following the example of European Community law, excludes from its operation 'undertakings which, by virtue of legal provisions, manage services of a general economic interest or operate a monopoly regime, insofar as this is strictly required for the management of the tasks conferred on them' (c.f. *European Community Treaty*, Art. 90(2)). Nevertheless, particularly because of the final words of this provision, the law will necessarily have implications for the public utility sectors: if nothing else, it will be necessary to adjust the laws relating to these sectors to take account of the role of competitive markets (and this was envisaged during the drafting of the competition law).

The final tendency concerns the pressures exercised by the European Com-munity, for the most part these are competition-oriented. So far these have had an impact in the sectors of transport, energy and telecommunications.

## PRIVATIZATION

There has been more debate on privatization than on deregulation. Here one can distinguish two phases; that of the 1980s and that which commenced during the 1990s. Many individual privatizations were accomplished during the first phase. This was possible because of the way in which the public industrial sector is organized in Italy. The sector is composed of three levels. First, there are the private law operating companies themselves in which there is State shareholding. Second, there are the public enterprises in the form of State holding companies; (*Istituto per la Riconstruzione Industriale*

(IRI), *Ente Nazionale Idrocarbi* (ENC), *Ente per il finanzimento dell'indus-tria manifatturiera* (EFIM) and *Ente autonomo per la gestione cinema* (EAGC)). Third, there is the Ministry of State Holdings, with powers of control, including establishing guidelines and scrutiny, over the public holding companies.

The initial phase of privatization applied only to the first of these three levels of State activity. It took place through the sale of shareholdings by the State holding companies; in some cases the entire stake of the holding company in a particular operating company was sold, in others only part of it. Amongst the companies transferred to the private sector, particularly important examples were the car manufacturer *Alfa Romeo*, sold in 1986 by IRI to Fiat; the *Lanerossi* group in the textile sector, sold in 1987 by ENI to the the private textile group Marzoto; and *Mediobanca*, a 'merchant bank' whose capital was held by three national banks in which the IRI was controlling shareholder. The three banks reduced their holdings in Mediobanca to a level equal to that of the private shareholders and thus the IRI no longer has control of the bank. Finally, *Cementir* was sold (on the basis of a 1991 decision of the Interministerial Committee for Industrial Policy (CIPI)) in February 1992 by IRI to the private Caltagirone group.

This first phase of privatization demonstrates six basic characteristics. First, the privatizations were never included in government programmes; this is the case for the Craxi Government (1983–5), the Goria Government (1987) and that of De Mita (1988). Second, the choice of companies for privatization was never made by government or by parliament; it was the State holding companies that specified those companies whose shares were to be sold. The decisions were then ratified by the Interministerial Committee for the Coordination of Industrial Policy. Third, the decision to sell was always made by the head of the State holding company and not by the Treasury or by other ministers. Fourth, the public enterprise had considerable freedom in deciding sale procedure. The only unifying factor was that the privatizations were approved by the interministerial committee. Otherwise, the negotiations were carried out by the holding company according to criteria established by itself. Fifth, privatization receipts were not paid to the Treasury, but to the public holdings themselves. Finally, these privatizations took the form of trade sales by public holdings to private groups, thus doing nothing to increase the holding of shares by individual private investors.

The second phase of privatization opened in 1990, and here one can identify three types of operation; the privatization programmes, partial privatizations and pseudo-privatizations.

# THE PRIVATIZATION PROGRAMME OF THE ANDREOTTI GOVERNMENT

Let us begin with the privatization programmes. The programme of the sixth Andreotti Government of 1989 set out their intention to dispose of public assets (and thus of shares) 'so as to contribute to a significant reduction of public debt and to introduce to the market assets previously unavailable thus releasing new entrepreneurial initiative'. A ministerial committee revealed in November 1990 that the public sector in banking, insurance and industry had a value oscillating between 100 thousand billion and 200 thousand billion lira (£50 billion to £100 billion). The programme of the seventh Andreotti Government in 1991 was more specific. It proposed the placing on the market of minority holdings of public enterprises, beginning with those of ENI and the electricity enterprise *Ente Nazionale per l'Energia Elettrica* (ENEL), and proposed the transformation of the enterprises into joint-stock companies. On this occasion, the receipts of privatization were destined to enter the coffers of the Treasury. However, this policy-inspired resistance by the holding companies who, through friends in the governing parties, expressed their opposition and demanded for themselves the privatization receipts.

These problems explain the slow and troubled progress of the proposal, which lasted throughout 1991. Finally, a decree law was adopted.[1] The law applies to the State holding companies, and to other public enterprises and State agencies. However, its scope is indicated very succinctly and treats together enterprises of quite different characters. This gives rise to the first difficulty.

The law proposes privatization in two phases. The first involves the transformation of public enterprises into joint stock companies. The transformation will be effected after a procedure involving a proposal by the Minister of the Budget, a decision of the interministerial committee, opinions from the appropriate committee of each house of Parliament, a decision of the board of the enterprise, and finally approval by the Budget and Treasury Ministers and also by the appropriate sponsoring ministers.

This procedure can only change the legal form of the enterprises. It shows, on the one hand, the final development of a tendency already confirmed; that of the reduction from three types of public enterprise (directly State-administered enterprise, public corporation and State shareholding) to a single type, that of State shareholding in a company form. On the other hand, it represents a regression because the State will become a direct shareholder without the intervention of holding companies, the model adopted during the first two decades of this century.

The transformation is designed to permit the sale of shares. This will constitute the second phase, itself to be effected in three stages: the disposal itself, the placing of shares on the financial markets or with institutional investors, and the attribution of receipts to the Treasury. The statute distinguishes the disposal of minority holdings (for which only the consent of the interministerial committee is required) from that of majority holdings resulting in a loss of control (for which a decision of Parliament and of the Cabinet are needed). The placing of shares on the financial markets and with institutional investors is to be achieved so as to assure 'the wide and enduring diffusion [of shares] amongst the public' and so as to avoid 'concentrations and dominant positions'. For the placing of shares to take place, a decision of the interministerial committee is needed together with a decision of the Treasury Minister. Finally, the latter minister will lodge the receipts in the Treasury. In the budget plans for 1991 receipts of 6000 billion lire (£3 billion) were anticipated, but these were not realized as the law had not been approved. For 1992 9000 billion lire of receipts (£4.5 billion) were planned.

This is not, however, the end of the problems and difficulties. In fact, after the adoption of this general law, which applies to all types of public enterprise, a further decree law provides that for the executive agency for the State monopolies,[2] a commercial body originating in the former State monopolies of salt and tobacco, the transformation into a joint-stock company can take place either by using the procedure already discussed or on the basis of a proposal by the Minister of Finance and a decision of the Cabinet. Trade unions for this enterprise, moreover, asked the Minster of Finance on 24 February 1992 to pledge himself to retain in State hands the joint-stock company after transformation. This request illustrates a widespread view amongst the unions, that privatization threatens security of employment.

The public enterprises have already resisted the implementation of the general privatization law. The *Istituto nazionale delle Assicurazione* (INA) has maintained that the law has no application to it because it has no assets capable of being transformed into shareholding capital. ENI and ENEL have made for their part representations to the government that they are not public enterprises of the conventional type but retain special privileges or monopolies (the former has a legal monopoly of research and exploitation of deposits of oil and gas in the Po Valley; the latter the monopoly of production and distribution of electricity). Thus the inplementation of this form of privatization programme has proved extremely difficult. A fundamental problem is that, on the one hand the government wishes to obtain privatization receipts to cover the budget deficit; on the other the public holding companies maintain that receipts must be used to finance their investment.

A second difficulty lies in the fact that some of the enterprises covered by the privatization law are not marketable. The railways *Ente Ferrovie dello Stato* (FS) record each year massive losses that must be funded by the Treasury. The situation of the IRI is only a little better. This raises a question: how can privatization be undertaken if private investors are not interested in acquiring shares from the sale of public enterprises?

By the middle of 1992, the procedures for privatization had taken few steps forward. The Interministerial Committee for Economic Planning adopted in March 1992 a direction in which it asked the enterprises to put forward a plan for their transformation into joint stock companies.[3] The plan must indicate their remaining tasks of a public nature, and those exercised under a State concession, and proposals for the disposal, finance, splitting, mergers and rationalizations of assets. The plan was sent to sponsoring ministers who will draft proposals for transformation, which will then be sent to the interministerial committee, which will in turn decide on the enterprises to be transformed and put into action the procedure for doing so.

Thus the first phase of privatization, that of transformation into joint-stock companies, has commenced; this phase is defined in the direction as 'in itself a stategic objective'. It is striking, however, that the law envisaged a simpler procedure, in which the interministerial committee would determine the direction of the transformation. Instead, plans have been requested from the enterprises themselves, rather than giving them instructions for their own transformation.

Further aspects of the direction are also of interest. Apart from the State holding companies and the directly administered enterprises, it is aimed at the electricity enterprise, ENEL, at the insurance enterprise, INA, and at the State railways, FS, and even at concerns whose industrial or commercial nature is doubtful (Institute for Foreign Trade (ICE), fair and trade-fair organizing bodies, and the Italian Society of Authors and Editors (SIAE)). Moreover, the enterprises are asked to indicate not only the method of their own transformation, but also plans for the sale of holdings in their subsidiaries. Thus the government has taken control of internal privatizations or those within groups (the first type referred to above), arousing still greater negative reactions amongst companies facing privatization (for example, in the ENI, which intended to have the companies *Snam* and *Agip* under its control quoted on the stock exchange, and which has seen the quotation blocked by the decision of the interministerial committee).

By mid-June 1992 replies had not been received from all the enterprises to which the directive had been addressed. Those that had not replied justified this by maintaining the necessity of a law passed by Parliament before the government could proceed, or else by claiming that the State did not contribute to their finances (this was so in the case of the Italian Society of Authors and Editors), or that their concern does not have a commercial character and is non-profit making (in the case of the trade fair concern *Mostra d'Oltremare*). The Society of Authors and Editors has even proposed bringing an action before an administrative court against the decision of the interministerial committee.

However, even the enterprises that have replied and presented a plan have observed that specific statutes are necessary for their privatization, or else have proposed the solution of retaining the public enterprise whilst creating a separate company for profit-making purposes, or have claimed that further State funding is necessary, thereby overturning the basic premise that privatization should be a means of gaining receipts for the Treasury. In order to resolve some of the difficulties that have arisen, a further decree law[4] has established that the public functions of the enterprises that will be transformed into joint-stock companies, will pass to the State, which will award them to the companies under thirty-year concessions; that the amount of capital can be derived, in the absence of the relevant fund envisaged by the law, from the estimated assets of the enterprise as valued by an official appointed by the courts; that the transformed companies will benefit from a privileged fiscal regime with a suspension of income tax, a regime already envisaged for the banking agencies privatized by the public credit institutions, discussed in more detail below. Thus the privatization programme, before it can bring revenues to the Treasury (assuming it proves possible to sell shares on the market), will be the cause of small losses of revenue.

In addition to all these problems, there are those relating to the trade unions and the Court of Accounts. Apart from the role of the employees of the State monopolies already referred to, those of the railways called a strike on 27 June 1992 against the privatization of the enterprise; in its public character they see a more secure protection for their jobs and perhaps also a guarentee of more 'liberal' treatment, with weaker discipline and less control on absenteeism. The Court of Accounts in its turn, in a decision of its section for the control of financial management of enterprises to which the State contributes funds,[5] maintained that its supervision must extend even to the new companies that will be created following the transformation of the public enterprises.

## THE PRIVATIZATON PROGRAMME OF THE AMATO GOVERNMENT

At this point in the privatization process, however, a general election intervened and a new government was elected. The new Prime Minister, Amato, put the programme of the government before Parliament on 1 July 1992, stating that 'my government will continue . . . the process recently commenced through putting into effect the measures already adopted [in relation to privatization] with the intention of improving them and completing them . . .' The improvement consists, according to the government, in privatizations 'that do not consist merely in the planned distribution of relatively few holdings to the benefit of a few purchasers and a few intermediaries'.

Under the new government the 'legislative dance' recommenced. In July 1992 a new decree law was adopted.[6] This overcame the difficulties that had so far hindered the privatization: the four principal State holdings (IRI, ENI, INA and ENEL) were to be transformed immediately and compulsorily into joint-stock companies. It was also envisaged in the new law that the Interministerial Committee for Economic Planning could determine that other public holdings, whatever their sector of activity, could be transformed into joint-stock companies. Oddly enough, the law did not provide for a similar transformation of other public enterprises not organized in the form of public holdings or operating companies (for example, the administrative or autonomous agencies of which the most important is post and telecommunications), although the new provisions have been applied by the interministerial committee to transform the railway enterprise into a joint-stock company.[7] The new legislation provides that the shareholder of the four State holding companies (but not of the *Banca nazionale del lavoro* (BNL) or of the *Instituto mobiliare italiano* (IMI)) is to be the Treasury, which will exercise its rights as shareholder by agreement with the ministries of finance and of economic planning, of industry, of commerce and of labour and of public holdings.

The new law, therefore, has a more limited ambit than its predecessor because, as has been noted, it does not extend to public enterprises that are not in the form of public holding or operating companies. However, it transforms immediately and compulsorily IRI, ENI, INA, ENEL and FS into joint-stock companies. The second part of the project, that relating to full privatization involving sale of shares to the private sector, imposes the following procedure. The Treasury Minister arranges a restructuring programme and, in conjunction with the ministers of finance and economic planning, of industry, and of commerce and labour, submits it to the Prime Minister. The latter sends the restructuring programme to the appropriate parliamentary committees for their opinion. Finally, the programme is approved by the Council of Ministers. The restructuring programme is, according to the law 'aimed towards maximization of the value of the holdings . . . also towards the facilitation of the disposal of activities and branches of the State agencies, exchanges of holdings, mergers and acquisitions and any other activities necessary for the restructuring . . . The programme must allow for the quotation of the companies created by the restructuring of the current holdings and the accumulation of proceeds for the reduction of the public debt'.

Finally, the plans of the new government envisage that activities specifically public and thus reserved for the State but allocated by law or by administrative acts to privatized enterprises are to be retained by the joint-stock companies, but in the form of State concessions.[8] Thus FS receives the concession to operate rail transport, and ENI the concession to produce gas in the Po Valley.

Following the transformation of the four public holdings referred to into joint-stock companies, they have adopted articles of association that contain important new provisions. In the first place, the number of members of the board is limited to three (thus excluding the participation of representatives of all the political parties in the governing coalition). Second, the shareholders (in fact, the government) have ample powers in relation to the sale and acquisition of companies, mergers, disposals, changes in form, etc.

The most recent developments have concerned other decisions relating to individual enterprises. First, a decree law[9] provides for the winding up, liquidation and consequent sale of interests of the *Ente partecipazione e finanzimento industria manifatturiera* (EFIM), whilst a further decree law[10] provides for the transformation into a joint-stock company of the executive agency for the State monopolies referred to above, with its production and commercial activities passing to a joint-stock company and reserving for the State functions and activities of a general public interest.

In view of these events, still by no means completed, the current situation may be summarized as follows.

First, five enterprises have been transformed into joint-stock companies; IRI, ENI, INA, ENEL and FS. In addition, it has been decided to transform into a joint-stock company the State monopoly agency. Finally, it has been decided to wind-up and liquidate EFIM.

Second, the implementation of these decisions has reached different stages. On the one hand, the decree laws relating to EFIM and the State monopoly agency have not yet been converted into full statutory form, while the other hand, in mid-September 1992, it was decided to privatize a bank currently owned by the IRI (*Credito italiano*) and an engineering company held by the ENI (*Nuovo Pianone*). However, the unions and employees in the latter enterprise are opposed to the privatization.

Third, because of the overlap between the laws, it is by no means clear which rules are applicable in each case. In the case of the most important public enterprise outside the scope of these provisions, the post and telecommunications administration, it seems that the privatization process may involve resort to the law passed by the previous Andreotti Government.[11]

Fourth, the current legislation diverges in two ways from that preceding it: the transformation of public enterprises into joint-stock companies has been implemented directly by law; and the law no longer contains specific rules and procedures for the sale of holdings that involve the loss of the overall State majority in the capital of an enterprise.

Moreover, compared with the original proposals of the Amato Government, the law adopted in August 1992 makes four backward steps. The first relates to the Ministry of State Holdings, which was to have been abolished, but now is expressly mentioned in the law. Second, in the original draft it was envisaged that a sale of holdings of between 20 per cent and 45 per cent of capital should take place quickly. In the final version of the law sale is subordinated to the accomplishment of restructuring. Third, in the original proposal, the decision to privatize was to be taken only by the government, whereas in the final version a procedure for parliamentary approval has been introduced on which the government's decision is dependent. Finally, in the original version, the text envisaged the creation of one or two 'super-holdings', to which would be passed the shares of the four holdings transformed into joint-stock companies. This would have rendered the process of privatization more manageable. However, it has been subsequently agreed that the shareholder of the transformed holdings companies must be the Treasury Minister rather than a new super-holding.

## PARTIAL PRIVATIZATION

Apart from these privatization programmes, during the second phase of privatization there have also occurred what can best be described as partial privatizations. This refers particularly to privatizations relating to credit institutions and to the postal services.

The 1990 law[12] envisaged the privatization of six public credit institutions out of about 100 savings banks and institutions of long- or medium-term credit. This is to take place in two phases. The first consists of the merging of institutions followed by their transformation into joint-stock companies, or the simple transformation of an institution into a joint-stock company, or the transfer by an institution of the assets of its banking business to a joint-stock company. In order to achieve this it is necessacy to present a plan to the Bank of Italy, to obtain the approval of the bank and of the Inter-ministerial Committee on Credit and Savings, and to communicate to the Bank of Italy the individual operations indicated in the plan in order that the bank can verify the conformity between these operations and the plan.

The second phase involves the sale of holdings. These are not subject to controls except where the majority of shares are disposed of. In this case an opinion of the Bank of Italy and of Parliament, a proposal from the Treasury Minister and a decision of the Cabinet are needed.

The 1991 law is more explicit.[13] This law provides that the Minister of Posts and Telecommunications may authorize the posts and telecommunications service to take holdings in companies in the posts or telecommunications fields or in complementary or related activities. However, the law provides that the administration must be in the position of majority shareholder. It is interesting to note that the posts and telecommunications service can also apply the decree law already described above.[14] As a result the service can choose between its own transformation into a company and the establishment of subsidiary companies.

In the case of the banks and of the posts, a transformation of the public enterprise into a joint-stock company is provided for. But State control over the company is retained; private capital may exist but only in the minority (this limit is fixed in the case of the posts but flexible in that of the banks as, with the approval referred to, even a majority of shares can be disposed of). The public enterprises thus become mixed companies, in part subject to ordinary company law but in part exempted from it (for example, they cannot be wound up). The second characteristic of these hybrid forms lies in the fact that the techniques adopted do not permit the Treasury to benefit from the receipts of privatization (with the exception of the case of the direct transformation of the public credit institutions into joint-stock companies).

## PSEUDO-PRIVATIZATION

Let us now consider the pseudo-privatizations. In this case the form only, not the substance of privatization occurs. Three examples have taken place. The first is that constituted by a decree law of 1991,[15] which provides that the Deposits and Loans Fund, part of the Treasury, can dispose of portions of its holdings in specialist credit institutions. In accordance with this provision, the fund has transferred to the Bank San Paolo di Torino its holding in the Credit Consortium for Public Works (CREDIOP). This is merely a financial operation, involving a shift of control over CREDIOP from the Treasury to the San Paolo Bank (the latter, in its turn, used to be a public credit institution, but has been transformed into a joint-stock company under the control of the Treasury). The fund has remained in the public sector, but the operation has permitted the State to inscribe the proceeds of the holding disposed of into its balance sheet.

The second example of pseudo-privatization can be found in the law relating to reform of the telecommunications sector.[16] The law provides for the abolition of the *Azienda di Stato per i servizi telefonici* (established in 1925 to manage part of the telephone services) and the creation by the IRI of a company 'all of whose shares are to be held directly by the said IRI'. To this company, according to the law, the Minister of Posts and Telecommunications will, after consulting the Minister of State Holdings, award an exclusive concession for telecommunications services for public use in addition to the installation of telephone services and related installations, currently managed by the State agency. This represents only a formal change within the State. The agency operating within the ministry of posts is to be transformed into a company whose shares remain, by law, entirely under the control of the IRI. The continuity between the current situation and that proposed in the law is underlined by the fact that employees of the State agency have agreed to become employees of the new company.

This final type of privatization, in fact, does not serve to raise revenues for the State or to transfer management of enterprises from public to private hands. The reasons for the changes are varied: to escape accounting constraints; to permit the appointment and management of staff on private enterprise criteria; to ensure the maximum managerial flexibility and to gain freedom from direct State control. Yet this is all without losing the advantages of operating in a protected environment.

## ITALY: DISTINCTIVE FEATURES

This analysis has made evident the difference between Italy and other European countries, especially the relatively undeveloped nature of the privatization programme in Italy. In other nations privatization, followed by new forms of regulation, has produced radical changes in the relationship between the public and private sectors. In comparison Italy has remained far behind. The reason for the institutional backwardness of Italy is to be found in the fact that 'pseudo-regulation' (in the sense that public authorities have reserved for themselves a vast amount of power which however they have proved in practice incapable of exercising) has been resorted to as has 'pseudonationalization' (the providers of services may be in form private, but in fact the overall position of the State through reserve powers, concessions and holdings produce an effect similar to nationalization). For this reason, the traditional arrangements have not been upset by the (very limited) deregulation nor by privatization.

Legal control remains marked by native characteristics; in order to avoid regulatory capture, enterprises are left to act in a predatory fashion and their actitivies are held legitimate by virtue of the public holdings in them. However, it makes little difference to the consumer or user whether the predatory enterprise is public, semi-public or private.

## DEREGULATION AND PRIVATIZATION IN A HISTORICAL AND COMPARATIVE PERSPECTIVE

In the light of our account of Italy, we can examine the problems of deregulation and privatization in a historical and comparative perspective.

If one examines the reasons for State intervention, one notes that 'market failure' or 'market defects' are at the base both of indirect public intervention (the State as regulator) and direct public intervention (the State as owner and manager); for example, control of monopoly, correction of 'spill-over effects', or 'externalities', compensation for 'asymmetric information', elimination of excessive competition. In some countries the alleviation of these 'market defects' is undertaken largely by regulatory means (for example, in the United States), in others largely by public enterprises. The structural variables that create pressure for the latter solution are principally two and these operate independently: first, the presence of social forces that support public ownership (for example, in Britain from 1945 to 1951, in France in 1945 and 1982); second, the absence of an independent administrative class, capable of undertaking in a relatively neutral fashion the task of regulation and supervision of private industry, without falling prey to influence by the controlled industry itself ('regulatory capture') or to political forces and the government (as in Italy after the Second World War). However, since the basic problems are the same whatever the solution adopted, the abandonment of one approach necessarily requires the adoption of the other. This is evident from Britain where, in the sectors of telecommunications, energy, water, and airports, after privatization the State has assumed powers such as licensing and price-setting. Apart from these means of regulation, the State has also retained modes of contractual intervention. The State remains present; only the form of its presence has changed. What appears as a withdrawal of the State, if one only considers ownership of assets in an enterprise, becomes a new form of organization and of action by the state if one considers public intervention in all its complexity. It is a transition from the 'positive State' to the 'regulatory State'.

An additional aspect of the role of the state concerns the relationship between politics, administration and the management of public enterprises. Only through this can one explain the different reactions of various countries to the same problems. For example, technical developments in the telecommunications sector have made possible deregulation in the United States and privatization in Britain and in Japan. Yet other countries, such as France and Italy, have reacted differently and have retained public management of telecommunications. This diversity can be explained only by the integration of public management in the political élite (in Italy) or in the administrative élite (in France); neither has been prepared to accept the loss of direct control over such an important sector.

A further issue concerns different types of relationship between State and market. This is a characteristic problem of the European Community, where, in relation to the creation of a single market, there is a certain obsolescence in the concept of the public enterprise dominated by the State. This obsolescence manifests itself in two ways. First, public enterprises are linked to the nation State, whereas the single market has a supra-national dimension (it is true that some national public enterprises exist with an international dimension, but only in certain sectors such as energy sources and to a limited degree, as they are primarily related to a national market and have objectives determined by national government). Second, the development of European integration has not been at the level of public administration but at the level of market integration; this has resulted in a strong accentuation of the role of the market, to the detriment of the main reference point of public enterprise, the State (for example, small private airlines put pressure on the institutions of the European Community to obtain observance of competition rules by large State-owned airlines).

If we now turn from the State to the market, privatization reveals two paradoxes. First, to permit the privatization of public enterprises, it is necessary to have a developed private sector and a strong financial market. Yet, especially in developing or partially developed nations, there is a strong public sector precisely because of the weakness of the private sector. The second paradox is that, in nations that have recently gained their independence, public enterprises are the result of a process of expropriation of foreign capital and of a programme of 'indiginization' of the economy. To privatize would serve to depoliticize the economy and would make up for a lack of management experience, but would return to foreign hands the control of sectors strategic for development. These two paradoxes explain the limited success of privatization in developing countries.

In a nation that is only partially developed (or, if you prefer, with a strong economic disequilibrium) and with a feeble financial market, such as Italy, privatization assumes a very different role from that in Britain or France and from other, less recent, examples in Germany such as those of *Preussag* (1959) and of *Volkswagen* (1961, 1965 and 1984). Whereas in Britain, in France and in Germany the enterprises have been acquired by small shareholders through a process of 'popular capitalism', in Italy the purchasers of privatized enterprises, have been large private groups (*Fiat*, *Marzotto*, etc.).

All these observations support the conclusion that privatization substitutes new problems for old. Whereas in relation to the public enterprises there existed problems of internal control, in the privatized enterprises there will be problems of external control. Instead of the problem of the autonomy of managers of public enterprises there will instead be that of access by public authorities to information on the conduct of privatized enterprises, and for the tensions created by pressure from employees of public enterprises in search of security of employment, will be substituted those created by consumers seeking improved public supervision of privatized enterprises.

## NOTES

1 Decree Law 5.12.1991, no. 386, converted without modification into Law 29.1.1992, no. 35.

2  Decree Law 21.1.1992 no. 14, article 8.
3  Direction of 25.3.1992.
4  Decree Law 26.5.1992, article 8, paras 6, 7 and 8.
5  Decision no. 23/92 of 16.6.92.
6  Decree Law 12.07.1992 no. 333, converted into Law no. 359 of 8.08.1992 and modified by Decree Law no. 365 of 14.08.1992.
7  Decision of 12 August 1992.
8  This provision replaces the Decree Law no. 26.5.1991, no. 98, article 6 already referred to.
9  Decree Law of 18.7.1992, no. 340, replacing the Decree Law 14.8.1992, no. 362.
10  Decree Law 21.7.1992, no. 345, replacing the above mentioned Decree Law 21.1.1992, no. 14, itself replaced by Decree Law 14.8.1992 no. 365.
11  Decree Law 5.12.1992, no. 386, converted without modification into Law 29.1.1992, no. 35.
12  Law 30.7.1990 no. 218 and Decree Law 20.11.1990 no. 356.
13  Law 30.2.1991 no. 412, art 17.
14  Decree Law 5.12.1991 no. 386.
15  Decree Law no. 151/1991, converted by the Law 12.7.1991, no. 202, Article 17.
16  Law 29.1.19, no. 58.

## BIBLIOGRAPHY

*Characteristics and history of public enterprise in Italy*

Cassese, S. (1962) *Partecipazioni pubbliche ed enti de gestione*. Comunita, Milan.
Galgano, F. (ed.) (1977) *Trattato di diritto commerciale e di diritto pubblico dell'économia*, vol 1 *La Costituzione economica*. Cedam, Padua.
Giannini, M.S. (1958) Le imprese pubbliche in Italia, *Riv. soc.*, 227.
Massera, A. (1978) *Partecipazioni statali e servizi di interesse pubblico*. Il Mulino, Bologna.
Merusi. F. (1977) *Le direttive governative nel confronti degli enti di gestione*. Giuffre, Milan.
Minervini, G. (1982) Le societa a partecipazione pubblica, *Giur. comm.*, 181.
Saraceno, P. (1975) *Il sistema delle imprese a pp. ss. nell'ésperienza Italina*. Giuffre, Milan.


*Public enterprise in Europe*

Parris, H., Pestieu, P. and Saynor, P. (1987) *Public Enterprise in Western Europe*. London, Croom Helm.
Timsit, G. (ed.) (1987) *Les enterprises du secteur public dans les pays de la Communauté européen*. Bruylant, Brussels.

## Privatization in Italy

Acocella, N. (1989) La privatizzazioni in Italia, *Econ. pubbl.*, 615.

Cassese, S. (1983) Le privatizzazioni in Italia, *Riv. trim. dir. pubbl.*, 32.

Cassese, S. (1991) Stato e mercato dopo privatizzazioni e 'deregulation', *Riv. trim. dir. pubbl.*, 378.

Cassese, S. (1992) Le imprese pubbliche dopo le privatizzazioni, *Stato e mercato*, 2, 235.

Del Canuto, U. (1990) Alcuni dati illustrativi dei mutamenti intervenuti nella struttura del gruppo IRI nel tempo, misurati a partire dalle variazioni della sua occupazione. In G. Bognetti, G. Murano and M. Pinchera (eds) *Scritti in onore di Alberto Mortara*. Franco Angeli, Milan.

Majone, G.D. and La Spina, A. (1992) 'Deregulation' e privatizzazione: differenze e convergenze, *Stato e mercato*, 249.

Schlessinger, P. (1992) La legge sulla privatizzazione degli enti pubblici economici, *Riv. soc.*, 126.

Vesperini, G. (1992) Privatizzazione e transformazioni dell'impresa pubblica in Italia, *Corr. giur.*, 1267.

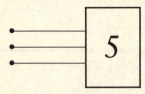

# PRIVATIZATION AND REGULATORY CHANGE: THE CASE OF CZECHOSLOVAKIA

## Michael Mejstřík and Milan Sojka

Thanks to its long industrial tradition and highly skilled labour force, Czechoslovakia (especially Bohemia and Moravia) had one of the most developed command economies in Eastern Europe. Compared to the developed market economies, however, Czechoslovakia is currently technologically backward and suffers a low level of labour and capital productivity. Competitiveness of Czechoslovak manufacturing has deteriorated, and since the beginning of the 1970s Czechoslovakia has experienced ever growing problems in selling its industrial products in Western markets. The structure of the economy became excessively rigid and was unable to respond efficiently to changes in the international market-place. An enormous misallocation of resources under the central planning system caused massive growth of unsaleable inventories on the one hand and vast shortages of consumer and capital goods on the other. Deep economic, social and political crises, whose symptoms had been growing all over Central and Eastern Europe since the beginning of the 1980s, erupted in the mid-1980s, and the Communist authorities were unable to solve them.

The dramatic events of November 1989 opened the door to a renaissance of political democracy and created the necessary preconditions for the country's transformation from a centrally planned economy to one based on market principles.

Systemic changes of the kind connected with the transformation of the former Communist centrally planned economies into market ones are unprecedented in history. The industrialized economies of the West created their market economies step by step over more than two centuries. Even Japan, famous for the speed of its development, needed a hundred years from the Meji restoration to establish a well functioning market economy. Czechoslovakia and other Central and East European countries are endeavouring to accomplish a comparable change in as short a time as possible.

The transformation process should be understood as a process of development that proceeds via trial and error as various policies are attempted, new obstacles encountered and solutions found. This process requires time, but at the very beginning some preconditions should be created for its further evolution. The market is a social institution which for its efficient functioning requires a whole network of other social institutions and regulatory bodies. The institutional framework encompasses a legal framework, distribution of property rights, government regulatory bodies, and various organizations representing the interests of different social groups, and so on.

The necessity of redistributing property rights in a post-socialist economy is viewed as the most fundamental prerequisite for a successful evolution towards a market economy and democracy. Its main aim is to create a dynamic market environment with an efficient competitive structure, able to enhance innovation and flexible adjustment to changing conditions of internal and external markets (see, for example, Blommestein and Marrese, 1991).

## THE TRANSFORMATION STRATEGY OF THE CZECHOSLOVAK GOVERNMENT

In Czechoslovakia the transformation strategy was worked out gradually during the year 1990, particularly in the autumn. The leading position in preparing it belongs to a conservative group of politicians and economists headed by Václav Klaus. This group prepared a complex programme of transition in a very short time span. The first set of steps of the transformation process was put in motion on 1 January 1991.

The core of this transformation programme consists of three main policy measures. First, macroeconomic stabilization based on restrictive monetary and fiscal policies; second, liberalization of price setting in internal markets and liberalization of foreign trade; and third privatization.

A major objective of the programme is to create an economic structure more or less equivalent to the standards of developed market economies. For Czechoslovakia, with its deep industrial traditions, it means reconstruction of markets, reconstruction of market property rights and a return to an efficient participation in international trade and integration processes.

The transformation programme rests on the idea, derived from the historical evidence of the developed market economies and modern economic theory, that without creating a strong private sector in the national economy it is impossible to form an efficient competitive economic structure, compatible with the economies of Western Europe and able to compete in international markets. Full membership of the EC, which is one of the major aims of the transformation process, is unthinkable without a strong private sector in the economy and without legal standards and regulatory bodies corresponding to existing West European standards.

In the past 42 years, under the Communist regime the State sector (with a co-operative sector as an appendage) became a completely dominant component of the national economy, exceptional even compared to Hungary or Poland. By 1 January 1991 the State sector, together with the co-operative one, was still producing almost 98 per cent of GDP. By the end of 1991 the share of the private sector grew to about 8.4 per cent, mainly in retail trade, services, and construction but with a very low share in industrial production (the most significant was its share in the polygraphic industry where it constituted 1.1 per cent). Even if we take into account the fact that our statistics lack effective means of monitoring activities in the private sector, any reasonable estimate of the size of the private sector for 1991 cannot give it more than 10 per cent of Czechoslovakia's GDP.

These figures only help to stress the enormous dimension and complexity involved in the process of privatization of the State sector in Czechoslovakia. Privatization on such a large scale represents a serious problem. This is the biggest issue in the transformation process in every Central and Eastern European country. The difficulties met in privatization in Poland and Hungary, the countries where the process of transformation started, show well the different conditions and dimensions of privatization in post-Communist countries in comparison to Great Britain or the other Western developed countries.

In Czechoslovakia, as well as in other post-Communist countries, we encounter a significant shortage of domestic capital, which might otherwise be used to privatize large State-owned enterprises. The market and corresponding legislation and regulatory bodies are only nascent. Even from the technical point of view privatization under these conditions represents a highly complex task if we take into account that thousands of State-owned enterprises should be privatized in a relatively short time. The bulk of these enterprises (70 per cent of State-owned assets) should be privatized, according to government aims, in three years.

The privatization process in Czechoslovakia has been developed in two stages. The first is the small-scale privatization run by special District Privatization Commissions appointed under the advice and supervision of the Ministries for Privatization and Administration of National Property of the Czech Republic and the Slovak Republic. The small-scale privatization concerns small-scale business units that are to be auctioned to persons or private enterprises. The second stage, and most decisive from the point of view of the success of the process of transformation, is the large-scale privatization of the big State-owned enterprises. A separate issue of privatization in Czechoslovakia concerns the transformation of co-peratives, which are especially important in agriculture.

## MAJOR METHODS OF PRIVATIZATION OF CZECHOSLOVAKIA

The existing legal norms presuppose three methods of privatization against payment: direct sale, public auction and public tender. These methods are usually called standard methods of privatization. Due to the shortage of national capital, coupled with doubts about the advisability and availability of foreign capital injections, it seemed pretty clear that the standard methods were not able to guarantee rapid privatization.

For this reason the so-called non-standard methods of privatization, including the free-of-charge transfer of State-owned property into the private hands of Czechoslovak citizens were considered. Finally, the decision to implement a voucher (or coupon) scheme for large-scale privatization was taken. There also exist free-of-charge transfers of State property, for instance to pension funds or municipalities. An additional important method of privatization, or more exactly reprivatization, is restitution of State-owned property to its former owners.

In the following pages we endeavour to discuss all the privatization methods used in Czechoslovakia in more detail. Our account is based mostly on the data for the Czech Republic, but until now the processes of privatization in the Slovak Republic have been evolving along similar lines with some minor departures. Different developments in the field of privatization may be expected now that the Czech and Slovak Republics have separated, but the separation is too recent to allow us to work out its consequences for the privatization programme.

*Small-scale privatization*

The small-scale privatization is based on two important laws passed in the autumn of 1990. The Restitution Act attempts to return, among others, the small-scale assets (real estate, barber shops, hotels, restaurants, etc.) expropriated without compensation in the last wave of nationalization in 1959 to their previous owners or their heirs. Where possible these assets are to be returned in physical form. The second law is the Small-Scale Privatization

Act, which aims at privatizing the remaining small-scale assets (new ones or those unclaimed by the previous owner).

In compliance with the Small-Scale Privatization Act, the assets involved are sold in auctions to persons or private firms. Since the beginning of the small-scale privatization, two rounds of auctions have been planned, the first for Czechoslovak citizens only and the second also open to foreigners. Public auctions organized by the District Privatization Commissions started in the beginning of 1991. The business units involved were (especially in the initial stage) often only rented, because the premises were located in State-owned, municipal or private houses and the house was not auctioned with the business unit.

The Small-Scale Privatization Act does not provide any definition of the scale of asset that should be considered subject to this statute. It only attempts to privatize any property that cannot be subject to restitution to the previous owners. Besides really small businesses, firms with several hundred employees were also auctioned during the small-scale privatization process. The decisions as to which assets are liable to the Small-Scale Privatization Act were fully in the hands of the District Privatization Commissions, whose members were appointed by the District Authorities. Hearing appeals against Commission decisions was the responsibility of the Ministry for Privatization and Administration and the National Property, or could be the subject of a court trial.

The small-scale privatization principally fulfilled its mission in the end of 1991 when most of the assets covered by the District Privatization Commissions were auctioned off. More than 22,000 businesses, in book value amounting to CKR 23.6 billion, were sold or rented. The proceeds from public auctions are transferred to the Ministries for Privatization and Administration of the National Property. However, the main objectives are connected with changes in property rights structures and not with raising funds from the process.

During the process of small-scale privatization a significant national small-scale private sector was created especially in trade and services. This helps to create more favourable conditions in consumer goods and services markets. In fact, the first steps towards creating a small-scale private sector were taken under the old Communist regime. The Private Shops Act was passed in January 1989, and since then Czechoslovakia has experienced continuous expansion in the numbers of private entrepreneurs (especially in retail trade and services). Until now, however, many of these have been only 'part-time entrepreneurs', because they maintained their jobs in State-owned companies and other institutions. So the number of persons registered as entrepreneurs does not tell us much about the real performance of the private sector. Major changes in the small-scale private sector development came with new legislation after November 1989, and especially after the Restitution and Small-Scale Privatization Acts were passed.

The process of small-scale privatization encountered some difficulties, and some unfair results occurred during its evolution. Limitation of small-scale privatization solely to Czechoslovak citizens was questionable. Czechoslovak citizens could participate according to the law, and the unit auctioned could be sold within two years thereafter only to another Czechoslovak citizen. Foreign bidders were only permitted to enter the second and subsequent auction rounds. Experience with public auctions during the small-scale privatization process indicates that on many occasions foreign capital participated via silent partnership in the first round of auctions, a process that probably drove auction prices higher.

The suspicion exists that some part of the foreign capital came from illegal activities: Interpol officially suggested to the Czechoslovak government that the way the auctions in small-scale privatization were organized allowed this, and that the opportunity had been taken, especially by Italian criminal organizations. Manipulation of auctions by organized gangs or collusive agreements, especially in small towns, aiming at reaching low prices via 'Dutch auctions' is also suspected, but our legal system does not provide sufficient base to prosecute activities of this kind.

The small-scale privatization programme represents an enormous social experiment the main objective of which was the creation of a new small-scale private proprietors class. The evaluation of the outcomes of the entire process could evolve in a more smooth and equitable way if the behaviour of banks towards people interested in becoming private proprietors was less conservative. The banks were not interested in business plans or entrepreneurial projects or skills of the applicants for credit, but in the ability to cover the credits by real estate or other property. The total amount of credits provided in the process of the small-scale privatization was, due to such bank practices, rather limited.

*Large-scale privatization*

The Large-Scale Privatization Act (the act on the conditions of state property transfer to other persons) was finally passed on 26 November 1991. Together with the Restitution Act it forms the basis for the privatization of big State-owned enterprises.

According to the Restitution Act of 1990, property nationalized after 25 February 1948 (the date when the Communist government was created and the Soviet-type centrally planned system initiated) should be returned to the original owners or their heirs. Restitution refers to the individual ownerships and partnerships only, it does not cover share ownership in private or public limited companies. Restitution was seen as part of a return to democratic and economic principles that promote the rule of law. It was a political decision. This decision was not favoured by the majority of Czechoslovak economists because of fears of complications, and the possibility of protracting the process of privatization. Government estimates assume the total value of the property to be restored to former owner or their heirs to be about CKR 300 billion ($11 billion) in book value.

Critics have stressed several major problems in the restitution process. First was the difficulty of finding former owners after such a long interruption of private ownership in Czechoslovakia, and the possibility of complicated court trials among heirs. Second, the descendants' ability to gather the financial resources needed to run the enterprise efficiently was questioned. Third, many properties may have been transformed after nationalization in a way that made it difficult to restore physically part of a functioning State-owned enterprise.

In fact these critical problems have only partly occurred. Restitution became the most rapid form of privatization and its negative impacts have been until now very small. Some problems nevertheless remain. Property can only be returned to persons residing on Czechoslovak territory. This condition is seen as unjust especially by Czechoslovak emigrants. There are continuous political attempts to push the restitution limit back to the end of the Second World War, or to enlarge the number of entitled subjects. The property claims of Germans from the Sudetenland who were under the Potsdam Conference conditions transferred from Czechoslovakia after the Second World War have also been revived.

In the process of restitution, the physical return of the property is preferred. In cases where it is impossible to return the property physically, the owners or their heirs are compensated financially, mostly in the form of relatively low interest bonds (5 per cent). Reliable figures on the restored property are not available. The deadline for restitution claims expired on 30 November 1991 but some complications due to unclear claims may arise.

The great majority of the State-owned enterprises should be privatized under the Large-Scale Privatization Act. This act refers to the privatization of several thousand large State-owned enterprises by standard and nonstandard methods in as short a time as possible. The major part of the large-scale privatization process is divided into two approximately equal waves (Report CVP, 1991). The first wave is in progress and should be completed at the end of 1992. The second wave is expected for 1993.

With the exception of some early direct take-overs, fusions or joint ventures by foreign capital (Skoda-Volkswagen, Sklo Union Teplice-Glaverbel, Rakona-Procter and Gamble, etc.), the large-scale privatization process started its preparatory stage in autumn 1991 and after some delay was finally set in motion in February 1992. The entire process is guided by government agencies. On the level of the federal republic it has been the Federal Ministry of Finance, and on the level of Czech and Slovak Republics newly created Ministries for Privatization and Administration of the National Property, which are responsible for the organization and control of the process.

Implementation is based upon individual privatization projects prepared by or for the State-owned enterprises. The managements of the State-owned enterprises selected for the first wave were legally obliged to submit individual privatization projects, but any other physical or legal person could also submit a 'competitive privatization project', designed to privatize the whole enterprise or parts of it. The Ministries for Privatization and Administration of the National Property of the Republics were able to choose between two or sometimes more privatization projects for the same enterprise. The original plan supposed privatization projects to be approved by the end of December 1991, but the entire process of preparation of the projects, and especially their consideration and approval, turned out to be far more complicated than expected and a delay of half a year occurred. The extended deadline for submission of the competitive privatization projects expired on 20 January 1992, the deadline for approval of the projects for voucher privatization being extended until the end of April 1992. An individual privatization project outlines the privatization method or methods used in the particular case, and decides the proportion of the book value of the property to be privatized.

Privatization according to law can be performed using the following methods or their combinations:

- direct sale to an owner known in advance;
- sale of the enterprise in public competition (on competitive bids);
- sale in auction (as in small-scale privatization);
- transfer of the property to municipalities or other bodies (pension funds, etc.) without payment;
- creation of a joint stock company (or some other type of business company) and its subsequent privatization via:
  (a)  sale of shares;
  (b)  using shares in voucher privatization;
  (c)  transfer of shares without payment to municipalities or other bodies.

Before the actual privatization of a State-owned enterprise can be executed, the property is transferred into a National Property Fund (Federal, Czech or Slovak). These funds were created by the law to take care of the privatized national property. They are not a part of the State budget and are allowed to operate only in the way stated by the law. These funds are satisfying restitution claims, obligations of the enterprises that are to be privatized, and so on.

During the process of preparing and approving the individual privatization projects some important problems have arisen. Because of the complexity of the process and the very short time schedules, for the most part only formal approval of the feasibility of the project can be granted, without any possibility of checking how far the existing management is profiting from the process.

## Voucher (coupon) privatization

Large-scale privatization represents by itself an enormous, highly complex social change with decisive impacts on the outcome of the whole transformation process of the Czechoslovak economy. The following data may clarify a little the dimensions of the large privatization process in Czechoslovakia. According to the official statistics the fixed capital value in the State property at purchase book value was valued at about CKR 3600 billion on 1 January 1988. Property to be privatized in the large-scale privatization process is estimated at about CKR 2800 billion. We should take into account capital consumption in recent years and large indebtedness of the existing State-owned enterprises (in February 1992 estimated at around CKR 200 billion). But even if we subtracted capital consumption estimated for recent years the remaing figure is still too large measured against available household savings, which amounted to nearly CKR 332 billion at the end of 1992.

Accounting value especially in a post-Communist economy does not say much about the real value of property and should not be exaggerated as a source of information for either the macro or the micro economic level. But under the present conditions it is very difficult and sometimes even impossible to value property by standard pricing methods used in developed market economies. It is done only in cases of selling the property to foreign capital where market valuation, usually elaborated by a foreign consulting firm, is required. In fact there is some discrimination against foreign capital which can buy former Czechoslovak State-owned property only on the base of its market valuation, whereas Czech and Slovak individuals and institutions can buy on the base of the accounting value of the property.

The above mentioned figures make it clear why the government decided to implement a voucher privatization scheme. It could in this way overcome the problem created by the shortage of national capital (or household savings). The political motivation for creating a broad popular base for the support of the transformation process was probably the most important incentive, but the possibility of very rapid privatization without the need to value State-owned enterprises at market values was also tempting.

The voucher (or coupon) method of privatization is based on the idea of free distribution of State property on an equitable basis. This method looks fair because the State property was confiscated from a wide spectrum of the population and was reproduced under the conditions of central planning by all the labour force (there is no way to determine how much any citizen participated, and how much he or she should be due). In a sense it is a just way of returning the property to its previous 'generic' owners. This method was seen as just because it provided the same chance for every Czechoslovak citizen over the age of eighteen.

Partisans of this method asserted that it was socially just and economically rational at the same time, because only the social élite with the best knowledge of the markets, able to create rational expectations and make correct decisions, would succeed in becoming real proprietors (shareholders) after some time. In this way State property would end up in the hands of the most able people. Thus the natural distribution of property rights could be achieved in the most simple and rapid way.

The voucher method functions as follows. From 1 November 1991 until 31 January 1992 each Czechoslovak citizen could buy a 'voucher (coupon) booklet' for CKR 35 and a 'voucher stamp' for CKR 1000 at any post office (this means for about $38). These amounts were charged only to cover the cost of the voucher privatization process as such, and have nothing to do with the value of the property distributed in this way.

Throughout Czechoslovakia several hundred local Registration Points equipped with a computer network were created and each Czechoslovak citizen aged eighteen and older could register his or her 'voucher booklet' with the 'voucher stamp' in his or her name. These registered voucher booklets were not negotiable and their validity is limited to the first privatization wave only. Any person with a registered voucher booklet was entitled to participate in the first wave of the large-scale privatization. Ensuring that everybody could register only once was achieved through the all-country computer network especially created for the voucher privatization.

The preparatory stage of the voucher privatization scheme ended on 28 February 1992 when all the participants were definitely registered (the former deadline having been extended).

In the last two months of 1991 when the process of registration had begun the public showed rather limited interest and the number registered at the end of the year was only around 500,000. The government had estimated the number of participants at round 4 to 4.5 million, and the average nominal value of property per voucher booklet roughly between CKR 50,000 and 100,000. Despite the minimal financial outlays and potentially high value of the property received in this way (the average annual pre-tax income in 1991 was CKR 44,000) the majority of the Czechoslovak population did not show any interest in this scheme. Some opinion surveys suggested that the public did not trust the voucher privatization method because of a widespread belief that only the low-performance enterprises with high debt and low profit expectations would be offered under this scheme and the best enterprises would be sold mostly to foreign capital. Really dramatic change only occurred from the beginning of 1992.

The number of registered persons grew dramatically in January and February, mostly due to a really aggressive advertising campaign by investment privatization funds, some of which had promised to purchase shares 'bought' with the voucher booklet entrusted to them after one year for a considerable amount of money. For example Harvard Investment Funds, the most aggressive investment privatization fund, had promised CKR 10,350 after one year, that is ten times the initial financial outlay of the participant. For the general public it was a signal that there was something to be gained from the voucher privatization. When the process of registration came to its end at the close of February 1992, around 8.5 million people had registered (from an eligible 11.5 million). At this moment the demand side was known, because every booklet gave the registered person the right to use 1000 investment points. To be able to determine the 'price' of the investment point the value of property offered for voucher privatization had to be fixed.

In the meantime, the individual privatization projects were prepared and approved. This was rather protracted and due to the length of the process the list of State-owned enterprises that were the object of the first privatization wave could be published only on 15 May 1992. (Only those enterprises with an approved individual privatization project could participate.) At this moment the amount of national property supplied for voucher privatization was known. The officially published list contains almost 1,500 enterprises with a nominal share value of around CKR 300 billion (this value was established on the base of the book value of the property).

The main principles of the voucher privatization process were the following. Every registered person had at his or her disposal 1000 investment points, which he or she was entitled to use in buying shares of the preferred enterprise or entrusting them to one of the newly-established investment privatization funds. Investment points function as nominal counting units (as a *numèraire*) in which the shares of State-owned enterprises offered in the voucher privatization are denominated. Initial prices of shares are established by the Federal Ministry of Finance according to the relation between overall demand and supply (that is, the relation between the total number of registered persons times 1000 investment points and the book value of the property offered for the voucher privatization in the first wave). For the first round a standard price of 33⅓ investment points per one share of nominal value of CKR 1000 was fixed. At this moment all shares had this nominal value. Prices of shares for subsequent rounds were determined by the Federal Ministry of Finance on the base of demand expectations for particular shares and outcomes of the round.

Any registered person could use their investment points in any of the privatization rounds. In every round the demand for shares met their supply and after the round was over the results of the trade were closed and published. In every round of the privatization wave we can distinguish four phases.

During the first phase the list of enterprises entering the round, their book value, the proportion of shares put into the voucher privatization, the number of shares offered in the round, and the price of shares in investment points are published.

During the second phase (which should last about three weeks) the owners of investment points should place their orders for shares. Each participant can order shares up to the amount of points he owns. The process of ordering is organized via post offices.

In the third phase (five days) the computer network of the Czech and Slovak Ministries for Privatization and Administration of the National Property processes the orders of the participants and matches them with the value of shares offered.

In the last phase (two weeks) the Ministries for Privatization and Administration of the National Property have to evaluate the resulting balance between demand and supply of shares for every enterprise, and inform each participant of the outcome.

The following outcomes are possible. The total quantity of shares of a particular enterprise demanded may be equal to, or lower than, the quantity supplied. In this situation all the participants ordering these shares are satisfied as they will receive the ordered number of shares at the price fixed in investment points. When the quantity demanded of a particular share has exceeded the quantity supplied, all these orders have to be rejected and the unsatisfied participants will receive back their investment points for use in subsequent rounds. The shares concerned will be revalued and offered at a higher price in subsequent rounds. Unsold shares of enterprises, where supply exceeds demand, are also revalued, re-evaluated and offered at a lower price in subsequent rounds.

These approximate steps in subsequent rounds should create favourable conditions for selling almost all the property offered in the wave of voucher privatizations. However, some extreme cases can arise. If in every subsequent round demand for particular shares exceeded supply the enterprise concerned should be transferred to the second wave or taken out from the voucher privatization scheme altogether. If the opposite situation arises and there is no interest in buying shares of a certain enterprise, it can again be transferred to the second wave or, in the case of enterprises with highly questionable prospects, can be closed and its assets sold in an ordinary liquidation procedure.

As mentioned above, during the preparation stage of the first wave of the large-scale privatization investment privatization funds were established. By 31 January 1992, 296 investment funds had been approved in the Czech

Republic and about 170 in the Slovak Republic (Havel and Kukla, 1992). The process of identifying what particular shares to order in the voucher privatization is highly complicated, because of uncertainty about the prospects of the great majority of State-owned enterprises entering voucher privatization. Historical book values and current profitability do not help to elucidate the level of future returns, and the process becomes more or less a gamble. As in Western market economies, an important part of the population is averse to taking risks. For these people the investment privatization funds offered both to manage the buying of shares for investment points, and the subsequent administration of their shares.

This aversion to risk, coupled with uncertainties concerning the valuation of enterprises, brought about a rather paradoxical situation in which financial intermediaries (institutional investors) received almost three quarters of all the investment points (72 per cent of all investment points in the first wave of voucher privatization). Taking into account the fact that some of the most important investment privatization funds were created by State-owned banks and other financial institutions (which are entering the large-scale privatization process) the process of voucher privatization took on an unexpected and rather strange new dimension.

The establishment and the subsequent activities of investment privatization funds were not regulated by any special legislation until April 1992. Their existence was based on the Large-Scale Privatization Act and the Guidelines for Establishing Intermediaries elaborated by the Ministry for Privatization and Administration of the National Property. Due to growing worries about the misconduct and risks of negative consequences for the whole privatization process, the Investment Corporation and Investment Fund Act of April 1992 was finally approved. This act considerably changed the operating rules governing the existing investment privatization funds. The funds are restricted in selling shares. Shares can be sold at the price level of officially agreed (by government authorities) stock markets. The investment privatization fund is not allowed to have more than 20 per cent of shares of one joint-stock company.

This new statute created particular complications for some of the larger funds. Many of the investment privatization funds were offering futures contracts (options) in the voucher privatization process. The first case was the above mentioned Harvard Investment Funds with its CKR 10,350 offer, but many other investment funds followed with similar offers of CKR 15,000, even CKR 18,000 after one year. The growing number of participants in the voucher privatization process put some of these promises in doubt. Average accounting value of the property per each voucher privatization participant fell to CKR 34,000 in the first wave and during subsequent years the market value of this property will be much lower – according to some reasonable estimates even under CKR 15,000 in the short run

(Kýn, 1992), and according to present and expected profitability of these enterprises we could arrive at estimates as low as CKR 8000 (Kápl and Tepper, 1992). The efforts of some of the major investment privatization funds to 'maintain the promise' could, if large numbers of participants try to realize cash for their shares in investment privatization funds, result in attempts to sell the shares in large amounts on the market, creating the danger of collapse of the emerging capital market in Czechoslovakia.

The risks involved and some peculiar activities of the investment privatization funds brought about the necessity of new legislation designed to regulate their activities. Probably one of the major errors made by the government during the first wave of large-scale privatization has consisted in letting the investment funds be created and operated without legislative norms for a long period (until April 1992); and then only after the game was well in progress enacting rules that considerably changed the prospects of investment privatization funds. On the other hand, without the advertising and futures contracts provided by some investment funds the voucher privatization scheme would have enjoyed only very limited success in attracting the Czechoslovak public, with considerable adverse effects on the overall process of privatization in Czechoslovakia.

The second round of the voucher privatization process ended on 14 August 1992 and according to official data 56 per cent of the shares offered since the beginning of the wave have been sold (in the first round it was 30 per cent). For subsequent rounds 44 per cent of offered assets remain to be sold (*Hospodářské noviny*, 17 August 1992).

## Major problems encountered and risks involved in the voucher privatization process

The process of voucher privatization looks quite appealing from the point of view of rapidity of change and the possibility of overcoming such intricate issues as the market evaluation of the State-owned property and lack of domestic capital. It may be considered from certain points of view also to meet criteria of social justice. But important doubts remain, stressed by many Czechoslovak economists. They concern the economic efficiency and economic consequences of the process.

Initial rapid change in the ownership of property rights through voucher privatization represents a formal change, but the creation of truly efficient structures of property rights requires time in which redistribution via the process of selling and buying the shares received from voucher privatization can happen. During this process the pre-privatization misbehaviour of existing management trying to enforce its interests will continue in many cases. The main objective of privatization, which is efficient allocation and usage of resources, may not be reached in the short, and perhaps even medium, term.

Voucher privatization may result in a very high diffusion of property rights, which in turn can help the present management (which frequently prepared their individual privatization projects with this aim) to become real proprietors whose activities will be concealed by the joint-stock form. If this is to become the major outcome of voucher privatization, it would be better, as the Russian economist V. Naishul suggested, to guarantee present managers of State-owned enterprises property rights and to privatize them in this way (Naishul, 1991). Sometimes the controlling body of shares can remain in State hands after the voucher privatization. (Because of high diffusion the controlling body could be really small.)

The effective control of new shareholders is very problematic owing to their lack of experience and skills. Even the investment privatization funds lack qualified personnel.

One common claim was that privatized enterprises would not receive any capital via voucher privatization or access to new technologies and know-how. This is of course true, but owing to the limited inflow of foreign capital there is no alternative method that would work better in this respect. (For foreign capital participation in the process of large-scale privatization in Czechoslovakia see table 5.3 of our statistical appendix.)

Some problems and uncertainties are connected with the role of investment privatization funds in the process. We have just mentioned the possibility of collapse of the capital market because of the activities of some of these funds. But there may be some other important consequences of their activities. Owing to the high share in the overall amount of investment points it is very likely that many enterprises will be controlled by the investment privatization funds. Some of the funds will not be able to control efficiently tens or even hundreds of enterprises because of lack of skilled personnel. In the near future many of these funds may have considerable shortage of liquidity (because of promises of buy-outs of their own shares and debts to the bank sector incurred by enormous outlays on advertising campaigns). It may force them to sell part of their shares, which will create significant surplus of supply and lead to low market prices, which could attract foreign capital. In this way foreign capital could buy quite cheaply important assets in the Czechoslovak economy. Another possible negative consequence of investment privatization funds' shortage of liquidity could be the pressure on enterprises they control to pay as high dividends on their shares as possible, whereas from the point of view of competitiveness these enterprises need massive investments in modern equipment.

High concentration of property rights in the hands of major investment privatization funds could lead to the preservation or even reinforcement of the oligopolistic structure of the Czechoslovak economy. This could enhance monopolistic practices typical of such market structures (see Klusák and Mertlík, 1992).

## NEW REGULATORY BODIES IN THE PROCESS OF PRIVATIZATION IN CZECHOSLOVAKIA

From the start of the reform process the Czechoslovak federal government and the governments of the Czech and Slovak Republics have endeavoured to regulate the entire process of changing property rights. The aim has been to avoid loss of property and spontaneous privatization via illegal forms of appropriation, fraud and stealing. The legislation created has not been ideal, however, and in some cases appeared only after considerable delay (as in the above mentioned case of investment privatization funds).

In order to make the process as rapid as possible, and socially acceptable from the point of view of social justice, spontaneous forms of privatization, similar to a modern 'enclosure movement', were restricted to a minimum. In this context we have in mind, for example, situations where managers of State-owned enterprises establish firms of their own and organize trade between their State enterprises and firms. They are usually using 'transfer prices' (high prices of delivered goods and services from their private firm to the State-owned enterprise and low prices for the products and services supplied by the State-owned enterprise to their firms). In this way assets are transferred from the State hands to private hands (see Klusoň, 1992).

To minimize such practices, and yet to achieve reforms speedily, the whole process had to be concerted and regulated from above. New regulatory bodies taking care of the entire process were created. At government level the Ministries for Privatization and Administration of the National Property of both the Czech and the Slovak Republics together with the Federal Ministry of Finance have prepared, administered and controlled the process of privatization. Their biggest problem, especially during the process of evaluating individual privatization projects, was considerable understaffing, which, coupled with demands for quick decisions, meant that approval was often a formality.

The small-scale privatization process was in fact decentralized via District Privatization Commissions. Their tasks were to select small-scale State-owned property for the process and to prepare and organize auctions. Their activities were under the control of the respective Ministry for Privatization and Administration of National Property. This part of the privatization process is now almost over, and these District Commissions were not allowed to participate in the large-scale privatization process.

In the Czechoslovak case, large-scale privatization is a highly centralized process that is implemented with the help of three new institutions. On the level of the Federal Republic and the national republics, National Property Funds were established to administer State-owned enterprises before their privatization. Their task is to prepare these enterprises for the subsequent privatization waves, transform them into PLCs, settle restitution claims, and help to solve indebtedness problems. These funds are not envisaged as entrepreneurial institutions, and they do not intervene in day-to-day management of the enterprises (after the system of central planning was abolished the State-owned enterprises were left to their own in many respects, the State practically ceasing to exercise its property rights). The funds are permitted to issue bonds and hold shares in banks and other enterprises.

For the administration of the voucher privatization the Centre for Voucher Privatization under the auspices of the Federal Ministry of Finance was created. Together with the Federal Ministry of Finance and both the national Ministries for Privatization and Administration of the National Property, it has prepared and organized the implementation of the voucher method. As we mentioned earlier, a computer network at registration points was also created for the administrative and technical side of the process; it does not play any independent regulatory role.

## SOME CONCLUDING REMARKS

Assessing the outcomes of the privatization process in Czechoslovakia is at the moment a very difficult task because we are now in the middle of the first wave of large-scale privatization. Change of this magnitude, using non-standard methods like vouchers, is unprecedented. This process will have crucial medium and long-term consequences, but for us it is difficult to see clearly even the main short-term contours of the outcomes. We can only hope that the legal framework for the large privatization will be able to create favourable conditions for suppressing the sort of spontaneous privatization that leads to high losses of property. It is also to be hoped that the rapidity of the change will help to create conditions in which the strange behaviour of State-owned enterprises waiting to be privatized (so called pre-privatization syndrome), which has led to many inefficiencies, will end as soon as possible.

New complications for the process of transformation in Czechoslovakia will arise with the disintegration of the Czechoslovak Federal Republic. Even if the current wave of large-scale privatization continues without interruption, the next wave will reflect the different priorities and outlooks of the Czech and Slovak Republics.

## APPENDIX

*Statistical summary*

The following tables are designed to give an overview of the arithmetic of privatization.

**Table 5.1**   Planned and actual outcomes of the voucher privatization scheme
*Planned situation – 1991*

| *Book value of property assigned for voucher privatization* | |
| --- | --- |
| From Czeck Republic | 140 bil. CSK (4.8 bil. $) |
| From Slovak Republic | 70 bil. CSK (2.4 bil. $) |
| From the sources of Federation | 50 bil. CSK (1.7 bil. $) |
| | |
| Total | 260 bil. CSK (8.9 bil. $) |

*Source*: Federal Ministry of Finance.

*Final situation – May 1992*

| *Book value of property assigned for voucher privatization* | |
| --- | --- |
| From Czech Republic | 206 bil. CSK (6.9 bil. $) |
| From Slovak Republic | 90 bil. CSK (3.0 bil. $) |
| From the sources of Federation | 3 bil. CSK (0.1 bil. $) |
| | |
| Total | 299 bil. CSK (10.3 bil. $) |

*Source*: Federal Ministry of Finance.

**Table 5.2**   Proposed form of privatization in case of all privatization projects

| | *Number of projects* | % |
| --- | --- | --- |
| Competitive bidding (public auction) | 1,150 | 10.5 |
| Public competition (tender) | 872 | 8.0 |
| Direct sale to an in advance selected subject | 4,905 | 44.8 |
| Transition to a joint stock company form* | 2,452 | 22.4 |
| Privatization of state's** property participation in other person's enterprise | 432 | 4.0 |
| Free of charge property transition | 887 | 8.1 |
| Voucher privatization (out of other forms) | 2,523 | 23.0 |

*Notes*:
* Enterprises where partial or full voucher privatization is planned.
** Enterprises where partial or full voucher privatization is possible.

*Source*: Ministry of Privatization and Administration of National Property of Czech Republic.

**Table 5.3**   Scale of foreign capital in key joint ventures

| In the manufacturing area | CSK m | USD m |
|---|---|---|
| Škoda-Volkswagen (BRD) | 11,496.0 | 383.2 |
| BAZ-Volkswagen (BRD) | 881.3 | 29.4 |
| Sklounion-Glaverbel (Belgium) | 875.4 | 29.2 |
| Technoplyn-Linde (BRD) | 519.6 | 17.3 |
| | | |
| *In the area of services* | | |
| EUROCHIM Bratislava | 221.5 | 7.4 |
| HOTEL INVEST Praha | 128.0 | 4.3 |
| Tourinvest Praha CBC | 41.0 | 1.4 |

*Source*: SBČS (Czechoslovak Central State Bank).

**Table 5.4**   Number of businesses sold within the framework of small privatization (Czech Republic)

| | Cumulated number of sold businesses | Cumulated auction prices (Mil. CSK) |
|---|---|---|
| **1991** | | |
| February | – | – |
| March | 228 | 88 |
| April | 1,349 | 914 |
| May | 2,948 | 1,525 |
| June | 4,749 | 2,696 |
| July | 6,478 | 3,898 |
| August | 8,016 | 5,288 |
| September | 9,514 | 6,879 |
| October | 11,201 | 9,790 |
| November | 12,911 | 10,130 |
| December | 13,230 | 15,621 |
| | | |
| **1992** | | |
| January | 13,935 | 16,869 |
| May* | 19,000 | 24,000 |

*Source*: Ekonom 5/1992.

*Note*: *approximate numbers (Ekonom 23/1992).

# BIBLIOGRAPHY

Blommestein, H. and Marrese, M. (eds) (1991) *Transformation of Planned Economies: Property Rights Reform and Macroeconomic Stability*. Paris, OECD.

Havel, J. and Kukla, E. (1992) Privatization and investment funds in Czechoslovakia, *REF/RL Research Report*, 1(17), April 24.

*Hospodářské noviny*, 17 August 1992.

Kápl, M. and Tepper, T. (1992) My a Penize, *Akcionář* (to be published in 1992 volume of the journal).

Klusák, M. and Mertlík, P. (1992) Transformation and Macroeconomic Stabilization of the Czechoslovak Economy, Conference Paper, Prague mimeo.

Klusoň, V. (1992) Alternative methods of privatization, *Politická ekonomie*, 1/1992.

Kýn, O. (1992) Trh, kupony a investični fondy. Praha, CERGE 1992.

Naishul, V.A. (1991) *The Supreme and Last Stage of Socialism*. London, CRCE, 35–6.

Svejnar, J. (1989) A framework for the economic transformation of Czechoslovakia, *Plan Econ. Report*, V, (52), New York.

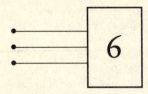

# 6

# PRIVATIZATION AND REGULATORY CHANGE: THE CASE OF POLAND

## Michal du Vall

The process of creating, or recreating, a market economy out of a command system is acknowledged to be enormously complex. The complexities of the task, however, are usually recognized in two forms: the *political* form of challenging and displacing the interests entrenched by the old command system; and the *economic* form of trying to ensure that new arrangements work so as to achieve desired objectives such as efficiency. But there is a third dimension to the privatization process, which may best be labelled the legal dimension. Privatization in a former command economy involves not only a change of ownership, but also the creation of legal forms of ownership. The special interest of the Polish case is that Poland, by virtue of its political history in the 1980s, has been in the vanguard of this process. Thus, the present chapter analyses, from a legal perspective, the recent Polish privatization experience.

The very essence of the transformation process in Poland is a change of the ownership of State enterprises. An important element of this programme is re-privatization, i.e. the return of property to its previous owners (or their heirs).

The aim of this chapter is to summarize current trends in Polish privatization. It must be stressed, however, that the legal acts are soon to be amended. Moreover, the drafts of new laws have also been prepared. Because of this, this chapter is based not only on laws already in force, but also on the drafts of laws still be implemented.

The legal bases for the privatization process are (or will be):

1 the Law on Privatization of State-owned Enterprises of 13 July 1990 (*Dziennik Ustaw* No. 51, item 298; this law will be amended soon);
2 the Law on Mass-Privatization and National Investment Funds (draft of 1992);
3 the Law on Reprivatization (draft of 1992).

Moreover the following existing statutes play an important role in this process:

4 the Law on Companies with the Foreign Capital Participation of 1991 (*Dziennik Ustaw* No. 60, item 253);
5 the Law on Counteracting Monopolistic Practices (*Dziennik Ustaw* No. 14, item 88).

## THE FORMS OF PRIVATIZATION OF STATE-OWNED ENTERPRISES

According to Article 1 of the Act on Privatization of 1990, privatization is based on first offering to third parties the shares of stock of a company resulting from the transformation of State-owned enterprises (capital privatization), and second, the sale or lease of all or part of a wound-up enterprise (privatization through winding up).

### Capital privatization

This form of privatization comprises two stages: transformation of an enterprise into a company owned exclusively by the State Treasury (so called 'commercialization' of an enterprise), followed by final privatization.

### Commercialization

Commercialization consists of changing the legal status of an enterprise without a change in ownership. It takes place through the transformation of a State-owned enterprise into a company owned exclusively by the State Treasury. The transformation is the result of a decision by the Minister of Privatization, made at the request of the Executive Director and the Employees' Council of the enterprise once they have obtained the opinion of the general assembly of the employees (delegates) and the opinion of the Founding Body, or at a request of the Founding Body (usually the appropriate minister concerned with the activities of an enterprise) submitted with the opinion of the Executive Director and the Employees' Council. A company owned exclusively by the State Treasury emerging from the transformation of a State-owned enterprise assumes all the rights and obligations of the transformed enterprise. All rights and obligations deriving from administrative decisions are also transferred to the transformed company. The activity of the company is subject to the Commercial Code of 1934 general regulations, unless specific provisions of the Privatization Act provide otherwise. A Supervisory Council must be established in a company, and one third of its members must by law be elected by the employees of the company. This solution seems to be some substitute for the present scope of self-governing powers of employees.

### Final privatization

As mentioned above, the establishment of a company owned exclusively by the State Treasury is just the initial stage in capital privatization. Final privatization takes place with the disposal of the shares (stock) owned by the State Treasury to third parties. Shares should be disposed of within two years from the date of recording the company in the commercial register. Foreign parties may also obtain shares in a company. This form of privatization started in November 1990, when the shares of the first five big enterprises were sold to the general public.

This form of privatization has one undoubted advantage from the point of view of the employees of the transferred enterprise: the opportunity given to Polish citizens of buying shares on a preferential basis, at a 50 per cent discount on the price offered on the first day of sale. However, the right to buy shares by employees on a preferential basis was limited to up to 20 per cent of the total amount of shares of the company held by the State Treasury. This rule will be amended soon, and under the amendment the employees will have the right to obtain up to 10 per cent of 'their' enterprise free of charge.

### Privatization of State-owned enterprises by means of winding up

This form of privatization relates to individual enterprises and seems to be more practical and advantageous for many enterprises than capital privatization. Privatization by means of winding up has been foreseen for relatively small enterprises. It opens up a wide range of possibilities for the assets of a transformed enterprise to be taken over, in whole or in part, by its employees, and not just by private domestic or foreign companies. As a result, the number of motions to privatize by means of winding up submitted to the Founding Bodies is currently growing rapidly. Winding up of a State-owned enterprise may take place either according to the provisions of the Act on State-owned Enterprises of 25 September 1981 (uniform text: *Dziennik Ustaw* of 1991, No. 18, item 80) or according to the provisions of the above-mentioned 1990 Privatization Act. In both cases the Founding Body of an enterprise is the decision-making body. In addition, both methods require the consent of the Minister of Privatization. The decision to wind up and liquidate is made by the Founding Body on its own initiative or at the request of the Employee Council of the enterprise. Finally, both the above-mentioned methods allow for the possibility of taking court action against the decision of the Founding Body. Liquidation of State-owned enterprises as provided for in the Act on State-Owned Enterprises of 1981 was meant as a practical solution in all cases where the financial condition of an enterprise could be regarded as poor. The purpose of winding up enterprises on the basis of the regulations of the 1990 Privatization Act is radically different. It is not the intention of the Act to create legal solutions for enterprises facing financial breakdown. Thus, according to the provisions of the Act, a Founding Body may rule that a State-owned enterprise be wound up in order to:

1 sell its assets, or integrated parts of the enterprise's assets;
2 use the enterprise's assets or integrated parts of the assets as a contribution to the company;
3 allow the enterprise's assets or integrated parts of its assets to be leased, against payment, for a specified time.

The sale of the enterprise's assets, or their integrated parts (plants, buildings, and so on) has the following features:

1 It should be regarded as the preferred form, taking into consideration the economic result and the financial needs of the State. The sale in question should be basically of a public character. It should also be preceded by the necessary announcements and take place on a public offer basis. The buyers may be both domestic and foreign companies.
2 The practical implementation of the solution may result in establishing, for example, a company involving the State Treasury as well as domestic and foreign partners. The form of the company can be either a joint-stock company or a limited liability company.
3 Privatization of an enterprise by means of winding up in order to allow the enterprise's assets to be leased, against payment, for a specific time seems to be the most attractive form from the standpoint of the employees. In the event that the value of an enterprise's assets is relatively low, this form of privatization creates the possibility of the enterprise being taken over by a company established by the employees. In practice, due to the small financial resources of employees, the process of raising the necessary funds to cover the required amount of share capital or the equity capital is a very difficult one; for this reason other domestic and/or foreign investors may also become the shareholders of such companies.

The establishing of a company that has successfully raised the required amount of capital is then followed by the next step in this form of privatization. This is the leasing of assets against payment based on a contract concluded in the name of the State Treasury by the Founding Body. The Privatization Act makes no comment as to the form of such a contract. However, the Act allows the parties to determine that, after a certain period of time, the user has the right to purchase the assets that he is using. In this context, the leasing contract is the most convenient one. There is not much experience in Poland of concluding leasing contract as yet. Moreover, no regulations are provided for leasing contracts in the Polish Civil Code. Nevertheless, this form is generally made use of in practice nowadays. In the concluded contracts the parties have to take into account, when determining the purchase price, the value of all rentals or other dues paid by the user to date.

*Mass privatization programme*

The Ministry of Privatization has prepared the draft of the Law on Mass Privatization and National Investment Funds. The programme of mass privatization should accelerate the transformation of Polish industry.

Accordingly, the specific form of privatization will be citizens' shareholding. The National Investments Funds (about 20 in number – hereinafter called 'Funds') will be created. The purpose of Funds will be to increase the value of their assets, in particular by enhancing the value of shares of companies held by the Funds. The Funds are to be created by the State Treasury in the form of joint-stock companies. At the beginning, the Funds will be wholly owned by the State Treasury. As soon as Funds are admitted to public trading on the Stock Exchange, all their shares will be made available to Polish citizens on an equal basis and for a nominal registration fee of about $25 (10 per cent of the average monthly salary). It should be stressed that each adult citizen will obtain the right to a share certificate representing an equal number of shares in all the Funds. These certificates will give Polish citizens the right for at least four years to trade outside the official market or to exchange through the intermediary of a licensed broker for one share in each Fund listed on the Warsaw Stock Exchange. For the purpose of large-scale privatization, about 600 State enterprises will be commercialized, that is, they will become companies wholly owned by the State Treasury (see above). The Minister of Privatization, acting on behalf of the State Treasury, will transfer 33 per cent of the shares in each such company to one of the Funds; as a result, such a Fund will obtain real influence over strategic decisions of the company. The Minister of Privatization will also divide among all the Funds on an equal basis an additional 27 per cent of the shares of each company.

Accordingly, 60 per cent of the shares in each company will be owned by the Funds.

The employees of each company will receive up to 10 per cent of the shares of each company for free. The remaining 30 per cent of the shares will initially be retained by the State Treasury for such purposes as providing income for the Budget, contributions to State pension funds or for other uses.

Each Fund must conclude a management contract with a different reputable professional investment advisory company, domestic or foreign. Such a management company will act to ensure the restructuring of the companies in which the given Fund will have a lead shareholding. This goal should be achieved by exercising the rights of a leading shareholder. The contracts concluded with the management company will provide that the main part of the remuneration will depend upon the financial results of the companies whose shares will be held by the respective Fund. Accordingly, the management company should have a significant economic incentive to maximize the financial results of those companies.

After the first few years of large-scale privatization, it is expected that the management company will gradually complete the phase of playing the active role in managing 'its' companies. After this phase each Fund should transform itself into a typical investment fund, being a passive investor in capital markets.

## REPRIVATIZATION

The draft of the Law on Reprivatization was finally prepared in 1992. The idea of the necessity of reparations for injustice seems to be clear. It is difficult, however, to find the proper way of implementing it. In particular, in most cases, it would be not possible to give the expropriated property in kind to the previous owners (for example, if the property is situated outside today's Poland). On the other hand the full indemnification would mean the destruction of the State budget. As a result, it is obvious that not everybody will be content when the law is in force.

The draft Law on Reprivatization was based on the following assumptions:

1 the reprivatization should be carried out speedily; accordingly, the scope of claims of the previous owners should be realistic and the procedure should be as simple as possible;
2 the previous owners should not be given full compensation;
3 the right to compensation will apply only to those whose ownership was expropriated with the violation of the laws being in force after 1944.

The compensation for expropriation is generally to be paid not in kind but in the form of capital coupons. Return of property in kind will be made only in exceptional circumstances and at the discretion of the state.

The reprivatization is to be limited to these previous owners (or their heirs), who are citizens of Poland and whose place of residence is that country. The citizenship of persons to whom property is to be returned is a very delicate and difficult issue. Although theoretically it will be possible for foreigners to acquire property through reprivatization (if they obtain Polish citizenship and start living in Poland), it seems to be obvious that such a solution will cause protests from many sides.

It is anticipated that the reprivatization claims can be declared for one year after the law is in force; afterwards they will expire.


## PARTICIPATION OF FOREIGN INVESTORS IN THE PRIVATIZATION PROCESS

There are many possibilities for participation of foreign investors in the privatization process, in general on the same basis as Polish citizens. Accordingly, the forms of such participations depend upon the kind of privatization. If the State-owned enterprise has already been commercialized (see above), the foreign investor may buy its shares.

If the State-owned enterprise is in the process of winding-up, the foreign investor may either buy this enterprise (or a part of it) or form a joint venture, in which the assets of the enterprise are a contribution of the State Treasury. Moreover, through negotiations with the National Investment Funds all investors will have an opportunity to invest in any of the companies involved in the mass privatization programme. Furthermore, as we saw above, the foreign managing firms should play a special role in large-scale privatization. In particular such firms are expected to be party to the management contract.

In accordance with the Law on Companies with Foreign Capital Participation of 1991 and the Commercial Code of 1934, such companies may take the form of a limited liability or joint-stock company. They can be established with a Polish partner or be 100 per cent foreign owned. The permit from the Minister of Privatization is required only if a company intends to operate in the following areas:

- operation of sea and air ports;
- real estate;
- wholesale trading in imported consumer goods;
- rendering legal services.

Since the Law of 1991 has been in force, the above-mentioned permits were granted for 1208 companies (about 25 per cent with German capital). The average level of investments (in cash or in kind) for one foreign investor was nearly 13 billion zloty (that is about $110,000).

There are the following incentives for companies with foreign capital participation.

First, an opportunity to transfer abroad:

- 100 per cent of profits, after tax;
- amounts from the sale of stock;
- amounts due from the liquidation of a company;
- remuneration of foreign employees.

Second, tangible assets representing a partner's contribution in kind to the company capital are exempt from customs duties.

Third, the Minister of Finance may, on receipt of a positive opinion from the minister concerned, grant exemption from income tax, when the foreign partner's contribution to the company capital exceeds the equivalent of 2 million ECUs and the company's operation are:

- to be conducted in regions of high unemployment; or
- will introduce new technologies; or
- will promote export of goods and services provided by the company to the value of minimum 20 per cent of its total sales.

It should be stressed that there is a uniform taxation system for foreign and Polish companies. The same applies to tax reductions.

## THE ROLE OF THE ANTIMONOPOLY OFFICE IN THE PRIVATIZATION PROCESS

The Law on Counteracting Monopolistic Practices (*Dziennik Ustaw* No. 14, item 88), deriving from its Preamble, is to promote market competition. According to the provisions of Article 11, the intention to merge and transform enterprises is always subject to notification to the Antimonopoly Office. The intention of establishing a company should be notified when it is likely to gain a dominant position on the market or when one of the parties establishing a new economic subject is in such a position. Within two months of the notification, the Antimonopoly Office may issue a decision prohibiting a merger, transformation or establishment of a company, when such a merger, transformation or establishment would give the subject a dominant position on the market. Pursuant to Article 2 of the antimonopoly law, there is a legal presumption of an enterprise's dominant position on the market whenever its market share exceeds 40 per cent. This presumption is rebuttable. If the Antimonopoly Office issues a decision prohibiting a merger, transformation or establishment of an economic subject, the Registration Court will refuse to enter the company in the register. In order to make decisions consistent, the Antimonopoly Office fixed in advance the group of State-owned enterprises that were monopolists and which before their privatization should be restructured.

In practice the enterprises having a monopolistic or dominant position themselves suggest to the Antimonopoly Office the mode of their division. On the other hand one should be cautious when dividing existing enterprises, as even big Polish enterprises are rarely so if compared with leading foreign companies. As a result, countries such as Poland should always take into account the European-scale background and the efficiency of existing enterprises. This privatization and demonopolization is particularly important in connection with Treaties of Association with the EC, signed between the Community and Czechoslovakia, Hungary and Poland, as the treaties oblige these countries gradually to reduce their import duties. It is obvious that in these countries there must be enterprises able to compete with EC companies. One can add that the Antimonopoly Office only has powers against monopolistic and dominant enterprises; it cannot prevent the splitting of existing enterprises which may be too small.

Difficult problems may arise as the result of the above-described mass-privatization programme. As a manager of each Fund will be from one leading company, it is hard to believe that there will not be a tendency to concentrate the industry and for collusion between enterprises forming certain groups. The role of the Antimonopoly Office in enforcing the Antimonopoly law will be very delicate, in particular because of the lack of foreign examples of privatization on such a scale. It is impossible to predict the future behaviour of managing companies and to react to this in advance by passing appropriate rules. In fact, nobody knows what the aim of such rules should be. In any case, a balance (whatever that means) must exist between the financial efficiency of the funds and the 'non-monopolistic' structure of the industry. An important role in this process will be played by the Antimonopoly Office, probably on a case-by-case basis.

This interim report on the Polish case returns us to our opening observation. To privatize is not only difficult economically and politically, but also difficult legally. Creating new legal forms, and working out the legal *process* of privatization is not a neutral, technical task; it interacts with, and affects, the political and economic interests at play in the process.

STATISTICAL DATA

It remains to summarize the scale of the whole process, as I do in the accompanying charts.

Until 31 August 1992, the process of transformation took place in 1841 State-owned enterprises (that is, 24.5 per cent of all such enterprises). Although hundreds of State-owned enterprises have been already privatized, the majority of industry is still in State hands. The essential changes that should bring about the programme of mass-privatization are due to start in 1993.

*Figure 6.1* Polish privatization summarized

| Forms of privatization | |
|---|---|
| Legal form of transformation of State-owned enterprises | Number of transferred enterprises |
| Winding-up | 1368 (in 415 the liquidation processes were completed) |
| Transformation into companies | 473 (183 enterprises were transformed for the purpose of large-scale privatization) |
| *Total* | 1841 |

| Size of privatized enterprises | |
|---|---|
| Number of transformed enterprises | Number of employees |
| 575 | 500 and more |
| 411 | 200–500 |
| 855 | less than 200 |
| 1841 | |

| Foreign investors | |
|---|---|
| Years | Number of companies with foreign participation |
| 1989 | 429 |
| 1990 | 1645 |
| 1991 | 4796 |
| 1992 (until Sept. 30) | 8860 |

*Source*: Information Centre of Ministry of Privatization

# 7

# ENVIRONMENTAL POLICY AND REGULATORY CHANGE IN POLAND

## Tadeusz Markowski

### THE LEGAL BASIS OF ENVIRONMENTAL REGULATION IN POLAND

Many different statutes and other legal instruments are responsible for the implementation of environmental regulation in Poland. The legal rules may either relate specifically to the environment or have an indirect effect through regulating other types of social and economic activity. In the first category are, for example, the Environmental Protection Act of 1980 (*Dziennik Ustaw* No. 3, 1980 as amended) and the Act on the Protection of Nature of 1949. By virtue of these Acts around thirty pieces of delegated legislation have been issued, not including specific decisions such as those creating natural sanctuaries. Thus, for example, the scope of the State Inspection of Environmental Protection (PIOS) is defined by a resolution of the Council of Ministers under the Environmental Protection Act.

However, the second set of rules, those indirectly protecting the environment, is much more extensive. Here we can once more distinguish two categories. The first regulates the management and use of natural resources, whereas the second regulates the powers and decision-making of public authorities. The first of these categories includes a large number of pieces of legislation such as the Water Act 1974, the Geological Act 1960, the Hunting Law of 1973, the Act on Toxic Substances 1963 and the 1986 Nuclear Act. Laws that affect the environment through regulating other forms of social and economic activity include the Acts setting out the fields of responsibility of the different organs of public administration, such as the Commercial Code of 1948, the Act on State Enterprise of 1981 and the legislation providing for State planning.

It is thus clear that in Poland there is no single and separate field of environmental law, and environmental regulation can emerge anywhere in the legal system (Brzezinski, 1975: 16). It forms part of a number of different branches of law, including administrative law, financial law, constitutional law, civil law and even labour law.

## INSTITUTIONS OF GOVERNMENT AND THEIR LEGAL RESPONSIBILITY FOR ENVIRONMENTAL REGULATION

The formal structure of the existing institutional arrangements, and the territorial organization of State and local government insofar as it relates to environmental protection, is shown in Figure 7.1.

The division of responsibility between the three tiers of authorities is as follows. First, there is the Minister of Environmental Protection and Natural Resources (see the Resolution of the Council of Ministers *Dziennik Ustaw* No. 63. 31.12.1985). This Resolution entrusts the minister with implementation of State environmental policy, with the carrying out of programmes for environmental protection, for nature protection, for water economy and geological works, and research and evaluation of the environment in general and changes in natural resources and their management. He is also empowered to issue rules relating to use of the natural environment, to secure observance of the law relating to the environment and related matters, and can issue other norms and standards in relation to pollution, nature protection, water management and geological work. Other responsibilities include the initiation and supervision of research and new technologies, surveying water resources, coordination and initiation of activities concerning endangered plants and species, creation of national parks and nature sanctuaries and a number of functions related to geological work.

Second, there is the Provincial Department for Environmental Protection and its territorial agencies, which, in the name of central government, also have a number of powers in the fields of environmental protection, water economy, nature protection and geology. These powers include granting permission for unusual uses of water, managing the Environmental Protection Fund, dealing with surface and underground water, taking the main responsibility in relation to flood protection, supervising geological works in their areas, imposing financial penalties for breach of environmental norms, supervising and controlling waste disposal and waste management and recycling, general coordination of nature protection within each province,

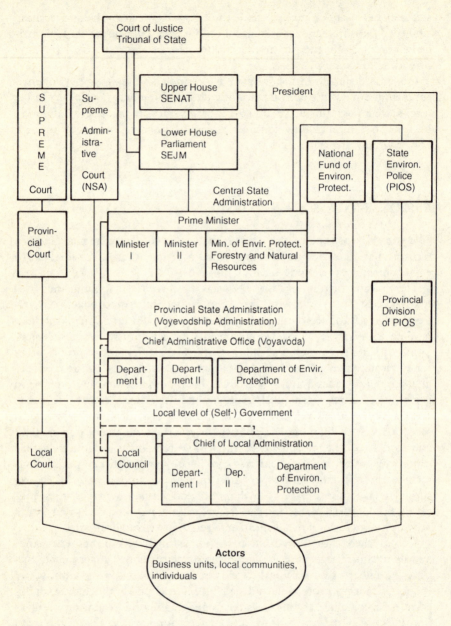

*Figure 7.1*  Institutions and govermental tiers in environmental policy system

supervision of national parks and general planning of the development of forestry and hunting, together with some specific powers to deal with extreme danger to the environment. In this case the chief officer of the province is authorized to take special action to eliminate the danger, including determining the duties of other public bodies to do so. A provincial subdistrict (or state territorial administration) has responsibility for other environmental controls on a number of matters, and for all matters related to the provincial water economy, including the registration of water boards and control of their activity.

Finally, local government (the communes) has both an inherent responsibility for environmental protection under the 1990 Act on Local Government, and any responsibility that may be delegated to it by the State government. Inherent responsibilities include restricting activities causing environmental distortion, for example by preventing building and prohibiting hunting and fishing, the administration of hunting, some responsibilities for forestries, forcing landowners to undertake preventative work against water pollution, flood evacuation, granting permission to cut down protected trees, controlling noise pollution, protection from waste and some decision-making powers as regards water law. Delegated tasks include orders for flood protection work and compensation for flood protection, certain powers of woodland protection and creating country parks.

## EVALUATION OF THE CURRENT SYSTEM FOR REGULATION OF THE ENVIRONMENT IN ITS SOCIAL, ECONOMIC AND POLITICAL CONTEXT

In order for us to understand the operation of environmental protection in post-Communist countries, it is important to understand the role of the legal system in command economies. Clearly, the legal instruments and institutions associated with the centrally-planned economy do not simply disappear when the decision to restructure the economy towards a market-driven system is taken by a non-Communist regime. This is a particularly marked difficulty because of the uncertainty as to which new instruments and institutions are required and the problems of how to move towards a more market-oriented system. It is not simply a question of the creation of technical rules but of how a new social system should be designed. This question raises difficult political and social considerations that are central in shaping the eventual form of transformation of the Polish economy. The meanings of the freedom and democracy promised as a result of the end of Communism are in Poland filtered through the deeply-rooted values and structures brought to economic management by forty years of Communist government.

The basis of the legal system in a State-owned economy is the ideology of central planning. This ideology treated the economy as a single consolidated system of functional relationships. It was assumed that within the system central government (or rather central economic management) would have complete access to all complex information on all aspects of economic activity and would thus be able to make optimal plans.

Once the centre had formulated these 'optimal development plans', the optimal plan would then be broken down into specific tasks and allotted to subordinate executive organs. These executive organs and economic units were then assigned the resources and means for achieving tasks assigned to them. Within this rationing system the role of legal norms was to provide access to the flow of information, to distribute means and resources and to create effective instruments of control. This was the ideology; the reality was very different.

Within this framework, the command economy was regulated by three types of legal instrument, the first two types of which can be characterized as 'managerial norms'. The first was included in various types of plan, and indicated the tasks to be implemented by economic units. The norms could have a directly or indirectly binding effect on the economic units addressed depending on the decision-making system involved.

The second legal instrument, also a form of managerial norm, comprised those norms linking the managerial centre of the national economy with other public bodies and enterprises. The legal basis for this type of norm was the hierarchical organization of the public authorities and the legal sub-ordination of production units to them.

The third legal instrument is composed of norms of a more general nature, based within legal disciplines such as civil and criminal law. However, the categories of such norms do not relate directly to the traditional branches of law, but are specific to the command economy. Thus in the command economy system there were attempts to create new specialized areas of law such as business law and public enterprise law (Wlodyka, 1982: 7).

The first two types of legal instrument have much in common. They are non-statutory or 'managerial' and apply within specific sectors of the economy. They do not correspond to the formal law of market-oriented countries, and are thus in tension with the third group, which is of a statutory or codified character. With such a legal system dominated by these 'managerial' or planning norms, there were as many types of regulation as there were different ministries and sectoral plans. Despite great efforts during the last five or six years to bring order to this law, huge numbers of regulations of this kind still remain and have not yet been eliminated.

The two types of managerial law described can be broken down further into so called 'planning norms' and 'directive norms'. These were highly specific and hierarchical in nature. Thus an essential instrument for the implementation of plans and of official decisions was the 'official order'. No procedural framework exists to regulate the freedom of a superior administrative body issuing such an order to a subordinate economic unit, and moreover the subordinate unit had no adequate rights of redress against decisions of its superior.

This legal structure was of great importance in shaping environmental regulation. Regulations concerning the environment could and can be found in any of the three types of legal instrument. In principle the planning norms should have been the highest form of law in relation to environmental protection, but this was not the case in practice for at least two reasons. First, the planning system had effectively disintegrated despite its central ideological importance. Second, short-term and narrow economic interests prevailed over environmental protection, and environmental controls only existed where their presence did not disturb the general goals of economic development.

Most instruments of environmental regulation belong to the third category of legal instrument. As a result, they do have some correspondence with the classical categories of law existing in market-based systems, based on the rule of law and an independent judiciary. However, the basic problem in environmental protection was the co-ordination of the three different types of instrument. In practice, the managerial forms of law prevailed over the general legal norms, and within managerial law the environment was peripheral to the interests of politicians and managers.

As a result, great inconsistency and particularism typified environmental regulation. Despite the existence since 1968 of the general Law on Environmental Protection, in practice such protection depended on the managerial law. The State executive bodies paid little attention to environmental quality for economic and other reasons. This official neglect increased environmental problems in all the Communist countries. A tacit purpose was to postpone investment in environmental improvement, and this, together with the plundering of natural resources, was one factor in enabling the Communist regimes to compete in international markets in certain periods without improving real productive efficiency.

The legal system as it affected environmental regulation was thus inconsistent and disintegrated, with many loopholes and weaknesses. This permitted decision-making processes to escape effective control. Thus a normal characteristic of the former system was the breaking of the law by ministries and the retrospective legalization of illegal decisions by new regulations, often offering as justification the 'social interest' of the society as a whole.

The transformation of the command economy into a privately-based economy will, of course, be a long process and, despite increased governmental and public awareness of this, there has been a growing consciousness that the roots of the former system are deeper than was initially thought. The legal system now has a hybrid character involving the law characteristic of the centrally planned economy described above, but also law evolving towards market solutions. The largest problem that has to be overcome in commencing economic recovery relates to the introduction of a relatively stable legal system and a privatization of the State sector so that most of the economy can comply with market-based structures.

Social barriers to the introduction of a new regulatory system include the fact that legal changes have very strong and visible distributive effects as regards the economic and social advantages of different groups. This polarizes society and results in the ad hoc organization of pressure groups and lobbies that resist change in order to retain short-term advantages that have often resulted from the inadequacies of the legal system that is to be changed. These tensions are to some extent reflected in the composition of the democratically-elected Polish parliament. The passing of new laws is strongly influenced by the conflicts of interest there, and laws are either passed after controversial debates or postponed for future resolution. Unfortunately the new environmental regulations are peripheral to contemporary political and economic concerns. As a result of this inexperienced democracy new laws are usually the outcome of compromise. This may be desirable for the political lobbies that have had access to the legislature, but not for the long-term good of the economy of the society.

A further aspect of the role of law in post-Communist society is also of great importance. Previously, law was an instrumental tool of State rule rather than an enabling regulatory system as it is in a market-driven economy. In almost all pieces of legislation there were loopholes leaving the decisions of bureaucrats unregulated. This is understandable where a single regime is responsible for directing all forms of social activity and the separation of powers is unknown, yet the diversity of social goals needing implementation created huge difficulties for the government. This attitude to law still shapes the attitudes of the new government, of private citizens and of business. Law is viewed as something that can be changed without difficulty if it is inconvenient, and that need not be obeyed because soon it will be changed. This is very dangerous when new regulatory systems are to be created, though the difficulties are perhaps an unavoidable side-effect of economic restructuring and the dramatic change in systems of values. The social costs of the post-Communist heritage and the costs of transformation have been unexpectedly great.

Reform of the legal system is directed towards a number of objectives. These are the elimination of 'managerial law', strengthening the regulatory role of the market, restoring the values of civil law, strengthening the position of the courts of justice, and gradually introducing 'soft' market regulation in environmental matters. However, it is doubtful whether the economy can be restructured by simply eliminating managerial law whilst the State sector remains different in nature from private actors. As a result of these difficulties, efficient environmental protection in post-Communist countries depends now much more on the functioning of the social and economic sphere than on even the best legally-formulated regulations.

## MOVES TOWARDS A NEW ENVIRONMENTAL POLICY IN POLAND

In 1991 the ministry of Environmental Protection published a Green Environmental Policy Document (National Environmental Policy, 1990). It was the result of a year of attempts to elaborate a targeted vision of an environmental policy and proposed a regulatory system in line with EC standards. The document clearly confirmed the weaknesses of the existing legal system. The Ministry proposed that 'under the changing conditions of the economic and political system it is necessary to incorporate the principles of sustainable development into the newly developed legal and economic framework as well as into the new system of economic management. The process of economic reconstruction now under way shall, in addition to social and economic goals, take into account environmental goals.' I here quote selected statements from the documents that will give readers some idea of the scope of the problems that Poland is going to face; needless to say, these will also occur in other post-Communist countries.

The first principle of the new environmental policy to be noted will be the rule of law. This will require the reconstruction of the legal system and its enforcement so that each regulation must be strictly complied with and no opportunity will exist for circumvention of the law because of 'circumstances outside one's control', 'the public interest' or 'impossibility'.

Second, environmental education will play an important role. 'The principle of common good shall be implemented through the establishment of institutional and legal conditions to be observed by citizens, social groups and non-governmental organizations. Action towards environmental protection will be promoted through environmental education programmes designed to induce a greater ecological consciousness and sensitivity in individuals and the public, and a new ethic of behaviour towards the environment.' As a result of this policy, in 1992 the National Educational Centre for Environmental Education was established. This centre is to develop a network throughout the country and assist other institutions in environmental education (Kruszwski, 1992).

Third, the 'polluter pays' principle will be adopted. 'In the transition of the Polish economy to the market system, environmental policy will be, to the maximum extent, subject to the economization principle. This means that the greatest possible advantage will be taken of market principles, with the necessary support of State intervention. The implementation of the economization principle shall take the form of strict implementation of the 'polluter pays' principle. This means placing full responsibility, including financial liability, for the effects of pollution and other damage to the environment upon its originator, the user of the environmental resources.'

Finally in the reconstruction of environmental law and in the system of economic instruments, the principle of decentralization shall be observed. This means:

1 extension (or introduction) of rights for local government and regional government administration to determine regional charges, standards and other environmental requirements in relation to commercial enterprises;
2 regionalization of national mechanisms and policies in environmental regulation in three kinds of geographical areas: areas of environmental danger, i.e. industrialized and urbanized areas, areas of great natural value (predominantly those with recreational functions, forests and 'environmentally friendly' agriculture), and intermediate areas (predominantly intensive agriculture and light industry, in particular the processing industry);
3 the coordination of regional policy with European regional ecosystems (e.g. the Baltic Sea and border ecosystems of neighbouring countries).

Underlying these principles, the duty to protect the environment is to rest on each individual and corporate entity. The public has the right to defend the environment and to organize to protect the environment. The government and self-government administration, which constitute the system of environmental authorities, are responsible for providing the conditions for implementing complete and publicly-acceptable environmental management systems.

The responsibilities and duties of State and local administration are set out in policy documents. Thus the central administration will have a number of main duties that will include the securing of public health, creating systems of environmental management, creating a coherent legal system for environmental protection, introducing economic instruments and mechanisms for financing environmental protection, and supervising environmental quality and creating a monitoring system. It will also be responsible for initiating and coordinating the activities of other administrative authorities and public enterprises and stimulating environmentally-related research and education, raising public consciousness of and sensitivity to the environment and carrying out international policy as regards environmental protection.

These responsibilities represent a recognition that whilst the economy moves towards a market-based system State intervention will still be required and that this domain cannot be subjected to market mechanisms alone. The government will also have responsibility for establishing technical standards to prevent the wasteful use of geographic space, raw materials and energy, and for promoting technical and structural changes to reduce the negative effect on natural resources of industrial and economic developments.

The main tasks of the provincial government (*Voyevodship*) administrations will be to monitor the environment, to apply the national policy on a regional basis, to issue administrative decisions based on environmental law and decisions of the central government, to supervise and inspect commercial enterprises and to coordinate activities for the protection of the environment in their own territories.

Below the level of central government, the territorial structure of administration will be developed in three forms. First, regional structures (above those of provincial administration) will be established with particular tasks assigned to them in relation to environmental protection. Second, the provincial administration currently possesses wide powers in the application of environmental law including issuing decisions provided for in that law. Their powers will be changed through transfer of partial control to the regional authorities in water administration and environmental monitoring, transferring some powers to local government (e.g. applying penalties, administering decisions relating to local enterprises, and some powers to dispose of funds), and by developing regional government's rights to pursue regional environment protection policies through determining standards stricter than those of the rest of the country, raising fees and penalty charges, deciding on the transfer of rights to use the environment, etc. District structures within the provincial administration will co-operate directly with local government.

The role of local government (communes) is to be augmented. The process will involve strengthening the commune's position in investment location procedures, not only as regards local investment but also in relation to projects of provincial and country-wide importance. They will also be granted full rights to participate in impact assessment procedure. Procedures will also be introduced to allow the commune to initiate or participate in decisions previously made by provincial or central administration, such as designation of natural monuments, reserves, communal parks and other protected entities located wholly or partially within a commune's boundaries, and also the tightening of standards and raising of fees and penalties above the level adopted for the whole country or province. Local government will also have powers to participate in the disposal of part of the funds paid by enterprises affecting the environment within the commune's area and to participate in the procedure of issuing permits to pollute the environment.

With regard to the non-governmental duties and the responsibility of economic entities themselves, the document states:

Holding users of the environment responsible for the resultant impact due to their activities is the basic principle for the environmental legislation presently under review. This principle will also be the basis

for practical enforcement of these laws and for the policy of government and self-government administration in environmental protection.
Responsibility shall be understood as a moral standard for the evaluation of the behaviour of citizens and economic entities, as well as a legal
standard with respect to material, civil and penal law.

Legal responsibilities will, in particular, include the obligation to remove
the effects of, or to terminate, activities harmful to the environment; to provide compensation for proven damage caused by individuals or corporate
bodies; to contribute to the cost of reclaiming the degraded environment as
provided by environmental law, and to ensure the payment of penalties
imposed for offences affecting the environment.

Finally, as regards the duties of citizens and the role of the public, it is
stated that: 'The duties of citizens with respect to environmental protection
are of a dual nature: personal responsibility for their own activities affecting
the environment and personal participation in the costs of environmental
protection through taxes or charges.' One particular item of note is that in
the new political environment and because of the strong role of the Catholic
Church in Poland, the policy document makes the following statement:
'The environmental goals are accepted within the framework of religious
doctrine. The influential power of Church institutions should be, to a
greater extent, included in the development of social behaviour that supports
the pro-ecological policy of the State.'

## THE LEGAL AND ADMINISTRATIVE TOOLS OF
THE TRANSFORMATION

Legal techniques are to be a basic mechanism for the implementation of
reform in Poland, and will be decisive as to its future shape and efficiency.
This applies equally to environmental protection. Of course, the efficacy of
legal norms of environmental protection will depend very strongly on the
role and functioning of the whole legal system and how the law is regarded
by society.

At present, complex amendment of existing legislation is needed in this
field. It has been considered most appropriate to draft a single comprehensive Act containing general principles and common standards for all forms
of environmental protection together with more specific legislation such as
a Water Act, regulations concerning forests, a hunting law, a mining law,
an ecological law and a building law.

The basic aims of the changes, in compliance with the recommendations of environmental groups, will be to achieve full coherence with other
elements of the Polish legal system and Poland's international obligations, to

adopt feasible and practicable duties and rights, and to express them in clear and explicit language. The main legal principles to be adopted will be, first, the principle of universality of environmental protection through the unified imposition of duties on all actors, including administrative bodies and any other organizations and physical persons. In practice, however, a greater degree of specification will be adopted for commercial bodies. Second, the principle of sustainable development will be adopted, as will be demonstrated in particular by the unequivocal statement that the duty of environmental protection cannot be treated as one that is in conflict with the interests of the economy, but which constitutes an element of proper economic management, whilst any activity violating that duty is absolutely unlawful. Third, environmental protection requirements are to be included in planning activities in combination with an augmented role for physical planning in the management of natural resources. Fourth, the principle of cost effectiveness will mean that environmental goals are to be implemented at the lowest cost possible to the public through the efficient application of market mechanisms. Further principles will be that legal or administrative limits on the scale of intrusion into the environment may not be exceeded even where the potential user is prepared to shoulder the burden of financial compensation (e.g. through a fine), and the principle that the responsibility for environmental infractions will be incorporated into a diversified and specified system of sanctions through civil, criminal, administrative and labour legislation. A principle of active public participation by citizens and organizations will be implemented through various forms of public inspection, the universal right to advance claims aimed at the abandonment or limitation of damage to the environment, and a universal right of access to information concerning the state of the environment and the means of its protection. Regionalization will require the transfer of a majority of decision-making powers to local administration leaving only general powers to central government, and the principle of local self-government will be observed through a gradual increase in the role of local authorities due to their strengthened position and greater expertise.

These principles will be included in new legislation; in particular, the following laws are now under preparation. First, the Natural Environmental Protection Law will regulate problems currently covered by laws on protecting the environment and protecting nature. Second, the Water Law will take into account in particular changes in the water management system, changes in ownership and the development of local self-government. Third, the Forestry and Forest Management Law will primarily stress the environmental functions of forests. The Geological and Mining Law will introduce changes aimed at the assurance of environmental protection requirements in the exploration and exploitation of mineral and forest resources. The Hunting Law will adapt regulations on game management, game protection and

hunting to the present requirements for the protection of forest flora and
fauna, and the State Inspectorate of Environmental Protection Law will
transform this institution into a strong, centralized body with broad rights
of environmental policing. Later on a further piece of legislation is planned
on extraordinary threats to the environment by adapting this to the legislation concerned with other threats to human life and health, and a further,
complex, act will be necessary in relation to all issues of waste management.

The operation of the State Inspectorate of Environmental Protection
(PIOS) will be adapted to the new organizational and functional structure
of public administration. It is envisaged that PIOS will be the source of
information on the state of the environment and on its users. The information will be gathered by its monitoring systems and made available to other
public authorities at State and local level and to public organizations and
citizens.


## ECONOMIC INSTRUMENTS

The category of economic instruments includes environmental fees, mar-
keted emission permits, subsidies in the form of direct grants, tax exemp-
tions and preferential credits, certain tax advantages, deposits for dangerous
substances, and penalties for breaches of permissible standards of use of
environmental resources. Drawing on experience from the most developed
market economy countries, these economic instruments will supplement
legal and administrative techniques.

The economic instruments will minimize public costs of environmental
protection through differentiating protection requirements; thus polluters
bearing the lowest costs for environmental protection should face the most
stringent standards. In practice, this principle will be implemented through
the issue of permits for the use of environmental resources and emission of
pollutants. These permits are to be tradeable. Thus the holder of a permit
will be able to sell it with the consent of the administrative authorities. A
secondary goal for the use of economic instruments will be the collection of
funds to be used for environmental protection. The fees and other economic
instruments will also provide a motive for such protection.

It is planned that the assessment, execution and utilization of depart-
mental fees will be decentralized. The imposition of an environmental levy
on fuels (a measure implemented or planned in some OECD countries) is also
being proposed. These funds are needed to co-finance national projects or
local undertakings that cannot be financed through regional budgets alone.

## CONCLUSION

The ambitious plans elaborated in the Green Paper are to be treated as visions for the long term, perhaps for implementation in the ten years or so before Poland becomes a full member of the European Community. However, experience has shown that legal changes in the field of environmental protection should evolve in conjunction with changes in the whole regulatory system and its institutional, structural and political context. For example, in November 1992 the Ministry of Environmental Pollution cut very high fees that had been introduced for polluters at the beginning of that year. Polish companies were unable to pay these because of the effect of the economic recession, and instead of providing a motive for environmental protection the fees put industries in an untenable economic position. This inconsistency between environmental policy and other regulatory policy and financial incentives had quite the reverse effect on environmental matters from that expected.

It has become obvious that the preconditions for effective environmental policy are more strongly dependent on the level of education in the society, its value system, its level of consumption and the economic performance of industry than on the legal regulation of the environment in itself. In redeveloping countries environmental policy should address preventative policy, cleaner production and waste minimization together with economic benefits to industry rather than simply developing the regulatory system to control environmental pollution. In the view of the writer, Poland should seek during the transformation period to develop its own environmental regulatory system rather than simply copying those of the developed nations, which, after all, might themselves change in the next ten years. This conclusion is confirmed by a study of the possibility of applying the British experience of privatization to the redeveloped countries (see Chapter 3). The whole British political, legal and economic environment was so specific that in spite of its great achievement by European standards, it is not comparable to the privatization efforts to be undertaken by the Central European countries. There is no historical precedent of restructuring that is replicable in post-Communist countries. This does not mean, however, that Western experience has nothing useful to show post-Communist countries. They can learn much, but learning does not mean copying; it means 'identifying what elements in a particular case are peculiar, and therefore unlikely to be reusable in other circumstances' (Chapter 1, p. 2). We should also consider in this sense the forms of environmental protection recently developed in Western countries in the form of 'soft market instruments' such as 'licences to pollute' and 'polluter pays' principles.

BIBLIOGRAPHY

Brzezinski, (1975) *Ochrona prana naturalnego srodowiska czlowieka.* Warsaw.

Kruszwski, S. (1992) *Wszystko o Krajowym Centrum.* Edukacji Ekologicznei, Aura no. 4.

National Environmental Policy Documents (1990), Warsaw, Ministry of Environmental Protection, Nov.

Sommer, J. (1990) Reforma gospodarcza – ochrona srodowiska – prawo, in *Skutecznosc prawa ochrony srodowiska w warunkach reformy gospodarczej.* Warsaw.

Vademecum w dzialnosci gospodarczej T 1,2, 1991, Slupsk, Saneko.

Wlodyka, Z. (1982) Prawo gospodarcze, Zarys systemu, czesc ogolna, Warsaw.

# 8

# PRIVATIZATION AND REGULATORY CHANGE IN HUNGARY

## Istvan Pogany

## INTRODUCTION

Privatization is frequently as much an expression of political values as of economic principles. In terms of the former, privatization in Britain has been associated with an emphasis on private property, with the fostering of an entrepreneurial culture and with the promotion of the broadly-based ownership of shares. In terms of the latter, privatization in Britain has been identified with improvements in the competitiveness and efficiency of industries, with the introduction of more effective regulatory structures, and as a significant source of revenue for the State (Veljanovski, 1987: 7–10). This dualism is apparent in the sometimes euphoric claims made by proponents of privatization who have argued that, in addition to its tangible economic benefits:

> privatization reflects a practical side of a growing view that the State has over-extended itself and assumed roles which are incompatible with an efficient and free society . . . Privatization redefines the role of the State and constrains it to a supporter of the market, which is a social organization where there is freedom to choose within the rule of law. It is this more than anything else which represents the radical character of privatization and it is this which is perhaps the most poorly understood.
>
> (Veljanovski, 1987: 205–6)

A similar amalgam of ideological and economic considerations underpin Hungary's privatization programme. However, for Hungary, as for the other former socialist states, privatization involves a cleavage with post-war economic experience that is much more striking than for any West European state. In Britain, privatization has represented, at bottom, a shift in the balance between the public and private sectors; a redrawing of borders rather than an ideological or economic revolution, despite claims to the contrary. While privatization has been acclaimed as offering gains in economic efficiency for British enterprises, such policies were not introduced at a time of acute economic and political dislocation.

By contrast, in Hungary, as in the other former socialist states of Central and Eastern Europe, the privatization process has come to signify a fundamental transformation of the political and economic structures that exemplified these societies for over forty years, an ideological as well as an economic revolution. Thus, privatization is now one facet of Eastern Europe's unequivocal rejection of the post-war programmes of wholesale nationalization, of the command economies and monolithic political systems that were imposed in the wake of Soviet occupation. At the same time, privatization has come to represent an affirmation of the values of private property and of entrepreneurialism, and of a commitment to the establishment of genuine market economies.

These newly-fashionable ideological imperatives are enshrined in Hungary's revised Constitution, which was substantially amended in the period 1989 to 1990 (see, generally, Pogany, 1993). Thus, the Preamble in the revised Constitution notes that Hungary is a state founded on the rule of law in which 'the multi-party system, parliamentary democracy and a social market economy are realised' (see Hungarian Constitution, 1949:XX tv., in *Hatályos Jogszabályok Gyüjteménye*, Vol. 1 (1991): 9). In addition, s.9(1) states that 'the Hungarian economy is a market economy, in which public ownership and private ownership receive equal rights and equal protection', while s.9(2) affirms that 'the Hungarian Republic recognizes and protects the right to engage in business and the freedom of economic competition'. These principles are complemented by s.13(1), which states that 'the Hungarian Republic guarantees the right to own property' and by s.13(2) which provides that:

> The expropriation of property may only occur exceptionally and in the public interest, in a manner and in cases specified by statute, and accompanied by full, unconditional and immediate compensation.

By contrast, the pre-1989 Constitution, which was adopted in its original form in 1949, was based on the classic Soviet, or more properly 'Stalinist', model. Thus, the pre-1989 text had declared that the Hungarian people 'are working for the complete construction of socialism', and that the

Constitution 'guarantees the achievements which have already been made and our further progress on the road of socialism' (Preamble, 1972:I tv., in *Magyar Közlöny*, No. 32, 26 April 1972, p.257).

However, Hungary's privatization programme cannot be understood solely, or even primarily, as a product of new ideological assumptions. It has also been a response to specific economic needs. Thus, the palpable short-comings of the Hungarian economy, even after the New Economic Reform introduced in 1968 and various additional liberalization measures adopted thereafter, provided the catalyst for more radical change aimed at the eventual creation of a market economy with inevitable large-scale privatization of State-owned assets.

The scale of the privatization process in Hungary, as in the other former socialist states, also calls for comment. In 1989, approximately 90 per cent of Hungary's national wealth belonged to the State. Thus, in seeking to privatize State-owned assets rapidly, as a basis for creating a genuine market economy, Hungary's government has been confronted with a situation that has not been experienced by any Western administration. As an influential Hungarian lawyer has commented:

> The governments of the western states have never had a task such as this. From an historical perspective, we are standing before an unknown road: from a so-called socialism we must arrive back at a different type of 'capitalism' from that which was forcibly abandoned fifty years ago. In addition, we must achieve this peacefully, using evolutionary means.
>
> (Sárközy, 1991: 18)

## ECONOMIC FACTORS UNDERLYING HUNGARY'S PRIVATIZATION PROGRAMME

As explained above, the objectives of Hungary's privatization programme have been twofold. In part, an expression of the new commitment to the creation of a liberal, market-oriented, property-owning democracy, the privatization programme has also been a response to specific economic needs. These are examined more fully in this section.

Hungarian economic policy, particularly from the late-1960s, was characterized by an increasing reliance on market principles, emphasizing flexibility and decentralization to an extent unparalleled in the socialist bloc (Bleaney, 1988, Ch. 6). State-owned industries were given considerable autonomy as were agricultural co-operatives, while agricultural production on privately-owned plots of land became an increasingly significant feature of the domestic economy. The scope for private-sector commercial and retail activity was progressively enlarged, while some of the essential legal features of a market economy were introduced, albeit in a rudimentary fashion.

Nevertheless, despite concerted efforts to marketize Hungary's socialist economy, these initiatives proved largely unsuccessful. Hungary borrowed heavily in the West during the 1970s to finance a large convertible currency deficit, while the competitiveness of Hungarian manufactures on export markets was progressively eroded (*ibid.*: 104, 109). Notwithstanding, the liberalization of the Hungarian economy, 90 per cent of the national wealth still belonged to the State in 1989.

It is against this background that the emergence of the privatization process must be understood, as a reaction to the economic cul-de-sac in which Hungary found itself, with its 'neither planned, nor market economy' (Tamás Bauer, quoted in Sárközy, 1991: 15). Thus, the economic reforms of the late 1980s, of which privatization formed an increasingly significant part, were inspired by the conviction, amongst progressive economists and politicians at least, that 'socialism, in terms of its economic structure, was unreformable from within' (Sárközy, 1991: 16).

Thus, privatization in Hungary was the product, at bottom, of a series of economic objectives. Ironically, these objectives had crystallized, and appropriate legislation had largely been enacted, *before* the holding of general elections in 1990, which led to the formation of a democratically elected, right-of-centre coalition government.

In essence, the objectives of reform-minded ministers and economists in Hungary, in the late 1980s, were to stimulate increased flows of foreign investment, to strengthen and develop the small private sector in Hungary, to free companies from the controls still exercised by State authorities, and to create a unified system of business structures available equally to joint ventures with foreign participation and to purely Hungarian businesses (*ibid.*: 98–9). By the early months of 1989, privatization had emerged as an additional, and explicit, aim of the reform process (*ibid.*: 104).

These objectives were enshrined in a series of statutes enacted by Hungary's unicameral National Assembly in the period 1988–90. The most important of these were the Act on Business Organizations and the Act on the Investments of Foreigners in Hungary, both of which came into force on 1 January 1989 (see, generally, Pogany, 1989: 56–61). These were followed by the Transformation Act, which came into force on 1 July 1989, and the Acts on the State Property Agency, on the Protection of Assets Entrusted by the State to Companies, and the Act on the Privatization of State-Owned Companies Engaged in the Retail Trade, Catering and Consumer Services, all of which came into force in 1990 (see, generally, Pethö and Jutasi, 1991, Chs. 7, 8). These statutes, will be examined more fully in the next section, with regard to their impact on privatization in Hungary.

## SPONTANEOUS V. STATE-DIRECTED PRIVATIZATION, AND PRE-PRIVATIZATION

Widespread agreement in Hungary on the need for privatization has not been matched by an underlying consensus regarding the appropriate means of privatizing State-owned enterprises. Apart from such technical questions, important policy issues have arisen with regard to *what* should be privatized, in what proportions and to *whom*. The 'what' question also raises the issue, dealt with more fully in the next section, of whether assets currently owned or controlled by the State should be returned to the natural or legal persons from whom they had been taken by the post-war Communist administration, i.e. whether they should be 'reprivatized', rather than included in programmes of privatization.

It is scarcely surprising, given the political sensitivity of privatization, particularly in the Eastern European context, and its inherent technical difficulties, that the modalities of privatization should have engendered conflicts. In the initial phase, culminating in the general elections held in 1990, privatization proceeded on the basis of the 'spontaneous' model. This may be defined as the privatization of a State-owned enterprise, whether in whole or in part, in accordance with the decision of the entity itself and on its initiative. As a commentator has noted, such privatization is 'spontaneous' only from the point of view of the State; for the State-owned enterprise that is being privatized, it represents a conscious and deliberate act (Sárközy, 1991: 97).

The object of the enterprise in seeking such spontaneous privatization was, particularly initially, not privatization itself. Instead, privatization was often incidental to the enterprise's primary purpose of attracting additional capital, or of acquiring modern managerial or organizational techniques (*ibid.*).

The 1989 Act on Business Organizations, mentioned above, was not concerned with privatization *per se*. Nevertheless, insofar as the statute facilitated the formation of business organizations with foreign participation, it afforded a firm basis for joint ventures to be established by Hungarian State-owned enterprises, on their initiative, with foreign partners (see s.4(1), Act on Business Organizations). The State property contributed to such a venture by the Hungarian enterprise was, in effect, privatized (Sárközy, 1991: 97–8).

In fact, spontaneous privatization, whether involving the transformation of part of a State-owned enterprise into a limited liability company (Kft.) or a joint-stock company (Rt.), or the establishment of a joint venture with a domestic or foreign partner, predates the passage of the Act on Business Organizations. MEDICOR, BUDAFLAX and a number of other medium-sized State-owned companies, which were already known in the West, chose this method of privatization in the period 1986-7 (Matolcsy, 1991: 188–9).

The 1989 Transformation Act, also referred to above, was of historic importance insofar as it provided, in part, for the transformation of State-owned enterprises into limited liability companies (Kft.) or into joint-stock companies (Rt.), regulated in accordance with the 1989 Act on Business Organizations (see Part II, Act No. XIII of 1989). While the Transformation Act was popularly regarded as permitting the spontaneous, and largely unregulated, privatization of State-owned enterprises, the statute actually imposed a number of controls that significantly restricted the autonomy of enterprises seeking to transform themselves into public or private companies (Sárközy, 1991: 109).

Nevertheless, spontaneous privatization, in its original form, came under increasing attack in Hungary insofar as it was seen to permit abuses, notably in the undervaluation of the State assets to be privatized. In placing the initiative on the enterprise seeking privatization, the danger presented itself that managers of such enterprises could be persuaded to conclude unsatisfactory deals with prospective foreign partners, whether through their lack of financial sophistication, eagerness to reach an agreement quickly, or through more positive inducements (*ibid.*: 100–1, 113). In part, the mounting criticism of the Transformation Act stemmed not only from dissatisfaction with its actual provisions, but also from its failure to *restore* the State's full regulatory powers over its enterprises (*ibid.*: 101–2).

The adoption by Hungary's National Assembly, in 1990, of the Act on the State Property Agency and of the Act on the Protection of Assets Entrusted by the State to Companies, brought about far greater State control over the privatization process. The latter act was passed precisely to limit the legal autonomy of State-sector managers who, as a result of the policy of increasing decentralization introduced in the 1960s, enjoyed very wide contractual powers over the assets of the State companies that they managed. With the steady erosion of the influence of the party apparatus at the national and local levels, of the ministries and of other public institutions in the closing months of 1989, while talks were held at the national level on Hungary's political future, the imposition of formal legal constraints to prevent possible abuse by managers negotiating spontaneous privatization transactions became essential.

The Act on the Protection of Assets Entrusted by the State to Companies preserved the principle of spontaneous or company-initiated privatization, while introducing a number of significant safeguards to prevent abuse. These included the requirement that, where the State-owned enterprise was proposing to contribute more than a certain proportion of its assets to a company, or to alienate land beyond a stipulated value, the enterprise was required to notify the newly-formed State Property Agency and to obtain a prior, independent valuation of its assets (*ibid.*: 113–15). The establishment of the State Property Agency (SPA), in accordance with the 1990 Act on the State Property Agency, extended the process of institutionalizing privatization in Hungary. The SPA, which was initially put under the supervision of the National Assembly, was given significant legal powers, thereby ensuring that company-initiated privatization was henceforth placed within an appropriate regulatory framework (*ibid.*: 117–18).

State-directed privatization emerged as a central feature of the new coalition government's privatization conception, articulated in August 1990. In part, the change of policy reflected the psychology of the period, in which everything had to be changed as part of the pervasive process of political, economic and institutional transformation (Csillag, 1991: 119). However, there can be little doubt that the coalition parties were genuinely united in their distrust of spontaneous privatization, while popular opinion was also hostile to the former government's privatization strategy. In addition, the Magyar Democratic Forum (MDF) the dominant partner in the new coalition, was ideologically predisposed towards active State involvement in economic affairs, while State-directed privatization was also anticipated by the passage, before the elections, of the Act establishing the SPA (see, generally, Sárközy, 1991: 121).

In a position paper published in August 1990, the new government made it clear that privatization of State assets would not proceed on the basis of a free distribution of shares. Nor would State property be returned to its original owners, with the exception of land. Instead, State assets were to be sold for a realistic market price, even if this meant delays in the pace of privatization (see, generally, *ibid.*: 122–3).

The objects of privatization had undergone a significant change. In Provisional Guidelines adopted by the SPA and formally approved by the National Assembly in a decision (*határozat*) in 1990, the reduction of the domestic national debt had become one of the primary aims of privatization (see 20/1990. III. 12 OGy. h.).

The government's policy statement indicated that the 'first line' of privatization would henceforth be State-initiated privatization. The SPA would be charged with drawing up groups of State-owned companies for privatization by various means, including a public offering of shares and by competitive tender. In large part, the privatization process would itself be 'privatized from within' with selected merchant banks or accountancy firms being invited by the SPA to provide their assistance (see, generally, Sárközy, 1991: 122).

The Act on the Privatization of State-Owned Companies Engaged in the Retail Trade, Catering and Consumer Services, which was adopted by the National Assembly in the autumn of 1990, stipulated that the privatization of these enterprises was to be initiated by the SPA (s.2(1), Act LXXIV, 1990). Thus, it was to form part of the new 'first line' of State-initiated privatization. Significantly, only Hungarian natural persons, and certain types of business organizations composed exclusively of Hungarian nationals, were eligible to take part in this privatization programme (*ibid.*:

s.8(1)), which is generally referred to as 'pre-privatisation' in the Hungarian literature. The decision to exclude foreigners was made feasible by the relatively small capital sums required to purchase the catering and other concerns covered by the Act. The exclusion of foreigners was considered politically prudent because of their preponderance in the first wave of spontaneous privatization from 1989 to 1990 (Matolcsy, 1991: 206).

The coalition government's 1990 policy statement indicated that the 'second line' of privatization would remain company-initiated privatization. However, the State would exercise 'increased supervision' over this process. In effect, it was envisaged that while State-owned companies could devise their own privatization packages, the SPA would examine these and make a final decision on each proposal, introducing such modifications as it saw fit and appointing an outside body to carry out privatization where necessary (Sárközy, 1991: 123). Evidently, this scheme left little of the original conception of spontaneous privatization in place.

## PRIVATIZATION V. REPRIVATIZATION

The efforts of the new administration to establish a more structured and centrally-regulated privatization programme were rapidly overshadowed by the growing political storm over reprivatisation (Matolcsy, 1991: 80). A significant body of opinion, with particularly strong support in the provinces, favoured the restitution of agricultural land to its former owners, reversing the confiscatory measures adopted by the State during the Communist period. Paradoxically, democratization in Hungary had both liberated political forces that had long remained dormant and had established new political and legal institutions that were capable, potentially, of threatening the 'efficient' conduct of economic affairs favoured by the proponents of privatization.

As indicated above, privatization offered the hope of significant capital injections for medium- and large-scale Hungarian enterprises, as well as access to new technology, management skills and marketing methods. In addition, privatization came to be seen as a significant source of revenue for the State at a time of acute budgetary constraints. These aims were expressly stated in the SPA's literature, issued in September 1990, when it launched the 'First Privatization Programme'. This programme represented the first stage of the new administration's State-initiated privatization strategy (see First Privatization Programme 1990).

However, the government that was formed after the elections in March 1990 represented a coalition between the Magyar Democratic Forum (MDF), the largest single party in the new Parliament, the smaller Christian Democrat People's Party and the Independent Smallholders' Party. The Independent Smallholders, who had secured just under 12 per cent of the votes cast in the election, agreed to join the coalition on the understanding that the government would ensure the passage of legislation to restore agricultural land to its former owners, removing the socially and economically damaging effects of the post-war collectivization of agriculture (see, generally, Fricz, 1992: 110–12).

The Prime Minister and MDF leader, Jozsef Antall, who was reluctant to introduce the necessary draft legislation in the National Assembly, sought a preliminary ruling from the newly-established Constitutional Court on the constitutionality of measures aimed at the reprivatization of land and the provision of partial compensation to the former owners of other assets expropriated by the State during the Communist era. The court, which was established in January 1990 as part of a comprehensive package of political and legal reforms, stated that it would amount to 'injurious discrimination' contrary to s.70/A of the Constitution if agricultural land were reprivatized, i.e. restored to its original owners, while other forms of property, which had also been expropriated in the same period, were not eligible for reprivatization (see 21/1990. (X. 4.) AB *határozat*, in *Az Alkotmánybíróság Határozatai*, 1990: 73, 79). Section 70/A of the Constitution, on which the court relied, provides:

> The Hungarian Republic assures to everyone residing on its territory human and citizens' rights, without any form of discrimination based on race, colour, sex, language, religion, political or other opinions, national or social origins, wealth, ancestry, or any other factors.

In addition, the court based its findings on provisions of the revised Constitution that guarantee the right to own property (s.13(1)) and that emphasize the rights of co-operatives, provided they are 'based on voluntary association' (s.12(1)). Thus, in rejecting the legitimacy of forcibly taking agricultural land from the co-operatives in order to restore it to its former owners, the court held (see 21/1990. (X. 4.) AB *határozat*, in *Az Alkotmánybíróság Határozatai*, 1990: 73, 80):

> In accordance with s.12(1) of the Constitution, the State supports co-operatives based on voluntary association, and recognizes the independence of co-operatives. This provision of the Constitution thus applies to co-operatives which, independently of the circumstances in which they were founded, exist on the basis of voluntary association. The only competent authority to decide whether or not a co-operative is a truly voluntary association is the assembly composed of the members of a co-operative. On the basis of these considerations, the Constitutional Court could not see a constitutional justification for the agricultural co-operatives to be deprived by statute, with general effect, of the guaranteed protection afforded by s.12(1) of the Constitution.

Crucially, the court's finding placed the agricultural co-operatives, provided that they were operating on a voluntary basis, under the protection of the Constitution. Thus, the court stated that, taken together, ss.12(1) and 13(1) mean that 'the Hungarian Republic guarantees the right to own property, including the right of agricultural co-operatives over their agricultural land' (*ibid*.: 81). In addition, the court held that (*ibid*.: 82):

> to deprive the co-operatives of their property, albeit in accordance with statute, infringes s.12(1) and s.13(1) of the Constitution, in the absence of prompt, unconditional and full compensation.

Following a further reference to the Constitutional Court, by the President of the Republic, the National Assembly enacted legislation that, in effect, permits expropriated landowners or their descendants to acquire land from agricultural co-operatives, albeit on payment of 'compensation vouchers' to the co-operatives and subject to various stringent requirements (see 1991: XXV tv., in *Magyar Közlöny*, 11 July, 1991, No. 77). Hungarian citizens who lost assets other than land, in government takings after 8 June 1949, were also entitled to compensation vouchers under the Act. In addition, such persons were given priority in purchasing (or repurchasing) their former property if it were offered for sale by the SPA or by a local authority (s.9, Act No. XXV, 1991). The principle of compensation by means of vouchers was extended further by the government, as a result of a reference to the Constitutional Court, to include citizens who were deprived of assets in government takings between 1 May 1939 and 8 June 1949, covering the most pernicious anti-Jewish legislation and post-war anti-German statutes.

The first decision of the Constitutional Court, referred to above, is also noteworthy for its finding that no one has a 'subjective right' to 'privatization' or to 'reprivatization', independently of decisions taken by the State establishing such entitlements (see 21/1990. (X. 4.) AB *határozat*, in *Az Alkotmánybíróság Határozatai*, 1990: 73, 76). In addition, the court held that the State is *not* under a duty to furnish 'partial compensation' to anyone (*ibid*.: 77). The court stated that such measures of compensation as had been proposed by the government were founded solely on the principle of fairness, and that they 'depend exclusively on the sovereign State's decision' (*ibid*.).

Thus, the Constitutional Court has done much to resolve any lingering uncertainty over property rights in Hungary by confirming that neither restitution of former property, nor compensation for its loss, are constitutionally recognized rights. On the contrary, such policies are viewed by the court as, at best, discretionary measures instituted by the State. However, rather different issues have been raised by cases referred to the court in which it has been argued, with some success, that Hungary must also take account of the 1947 Paris Peace Treaty, to which it is a party, in formulating its compensation (and restitution) policies, particularly towards the Jewish community (see 15/1993. (III. 12.) AB *határozat* and 16/1993. (III. 12.) AB *határozat*, in *Magyar Közlöny*, No. 29, 12 March 1993, pp. 1567, 1598).

The decisions of the court have largely reinforced the previously declared policy of the government to confine any measures of reprivatization to the land. This policy, which was contained in the government's August 1990 position paper, and which has been only slightly extended by s.9 of Act XXV of 1991, has done much to reassure both foreign and domestic investors in the manufacturing, commercial and service sectors that any investments they made would not be placed in jeopardy by subsequent claims brought by former owners (Matolcsy, 1991: 80).

## ACTIVE PRIVATIZATION: THE PRIVATIZATION PROGRAMMES

In its August 1990 position paper, mentioned above, the new government cautioned against over-hasty privatization and ruled out the need for 'privatization shock-therapy' (Sárközy, 1991: 122). Nevertheless, it soon became the government's declared aim to reduce State property, as a proportion of the economy, from 90 per cent to 30–40 per cent within three years (*Heti Világgazdaság*, 22 September 1990: 86). The scale and complexity of the proposed task is made clear by the fact that there were some 2,400 State-owned enterprises operating in Hungary at the time.

With a view to achieving its stated goal, the State Property Agency introduced the First Privatization Programme (FPP) in September 1990. The programme represented a bold example of State-initiated privatization in which twenty State-owned enterprises, operating in the manufacturing and service sectors, were selected for privatization. The enterprises, which included well-known and potentially profitable concerns such as the IBUSZ travel company, the Hollohász porcelain concern and a number of major hotel chains, were selected on the basis of their recent economic performance, their readiness for rapid privatization and the favourable attitude of their employees. It was hoped that privatization, in addition to providing a welcome injection of capital, would also offer managerial and organizational expertise, as well as encourage domestic investors (*ibid.*).

In accordance with the previously-mentioned 'privatization of privatization' concept, Western consulting firms and banks were invited to tender bids to manage these privatizations. As the staff of the SPA numbered only thirty to thirty-five persons, in September 1990, such external assistance was clearly essential.

A Second Privatization Programme (SPP) was announced by the SPA in December 1990, with the declared object of privatizing a further forty to sixty State-owned enterprises. In contrast to the companies included in the

First Privatization Programme, the latter were mostly shell companies, the bulk of whose assets had already been transferred to joint ventures established with foreign partners (Sulkowski, Glick and Richter, 1991: 34). The State-owned enterprises included in the SPP were involved in various activities, ranging from textiles, light industry and construction.

A Third Privatization Programme has since been initiated. However, these 'active' privatization schemes, involving the sale of major enterprises engaged in important economic activities, have resulted in relatively few privatizations to date (Ashton and Cohen, 1992: 25). By contrast, enterprise-initiated, i.e. spontaneous privatization, and various other techniques, have been much more successful.

## SPONTANEOUS, INVESTOR-INITIATED, RETAIL AND SELF-PRIVATIZATION

As noted above, the establishment of the SPA and the passage of the Act on the Protection of Assets Entrusted by the State to Companies did not extinguish the practice of spontaneous, or enterprise-initiated, privatization. However, the legislation enacted in 1990 did introduce a number of significant safeguards.

Enterprise-initiated privatization, in which the management of a State-owned enterprise takes the initiative in concluding a provisional agreement with a prospective investor, involving the sale of equity in the transformed enterprise, remains a significant form of privatization in Hungary. Crucially, however, such agreements must be approved by the SPA, which may also take an active part in the negotiations (Ashton and Cohen, 1992: 26).

Investor-initiated privatization has also been developed as an alternative technique in which prospective investors, whether foreign or domestic, may approach the SPA with proposals regarding specific State-owned enterprises. The SPA, in considering such proposals, will discuss them with the management of the enterprise concerned and may seek other offers or appoint an external adviser (Sulkowski, Glick and Richter, 1991: 34).

Privatization of enterprises engaged in retail trade, catering and consumer services remains a distinct branch of the privatization process (see, generally, Pethö and Jutasi, 1991: Ch. 8). From the passage of Act No. LXXIV in 1990, referred to above, some 2120 such enterprises had been privatized by the beginning of 1992 (Ashton and Cohen, 1992: 26). As noted previously, foreigners are, in general, excluded from this sector of privatization that is directed, in part, at increasing the numbers of Hungarian businessmen and entrepreneurs (Pethö and Jutasi, 1991: 120–1).

'Self-privatization', which is also referred to as 'decentralized' privatization in the Hungarian literature, has been in operation since September

1991. Initially applicable only to small-scale Hungarian enterprises, it involves the privatization of such entities through the services of specially selected consulting companies and financial institutions. Some 433 enterprises were chosen by the SPA for inclusion in this first phase of self-privatization (Pethö and Jutasi, 1991: 114). According to the most recent figures available from Hungary, almost a hundred enterprises have been privatized in this way, a high proportion having been bought by Hungarian investors (*Figyelö*, 18 March 1993: 17). In addition, a much larger number have already been transformed into business organizations, thereby taking significant steps towards the goal of privatization. This process is now regulated by Act LIV of 1992.

A second phase of self-privatization was initiated in August 1992, applicable to some 300 medium-sized Hungarian enterprises employing up to 1000 persons each (*Figyelö*, 3 December 1992: 22). However, it is not anticipated that Hungarians will feature so prominently in this second phase of decentralized privatization.


## THE SCOPE OF THE PRIVATIZATION PROCESS

While recognizing that the State has 'over-extended itself', particularly in the post-war period, and that it has 'assumed roles which are incompatible with an efficient and free society' (Veljanovski, 1987: 205), it has also been understood that limits must be placed on the privatization process in order to protect important economic, security and cultural interests. Accordingly, in August 1992, the government published a list of 160 State-owned enterprises that would be privatized only in part, or excluded altogether from the privatization process. In a number of these, including the national oil company (MOL), the electric power utilities (MVMT), the national airline (MALÉV) and the State-owned shipping company (MAHART), the State was to retain 50 per cent plus one vote. In the manufacturing sector, the State share was set at 25 per cent plus one vote in various enterprises including Ikarus, Rába, the porcelain manufacturer Herend and in a number of chemical and pharmaceutical companies (see, generally, *Figyelö*, 3 September 1991: 1, 13). A smaller State share was retained in a number of paprika, salami and wine-producing enterprises, notably the producer of Tokaj wines.

In the cultural and educational sphere, various publishing houses were to remain wholly or partially in State-ownership, while the State was to retain a 25 per cent share plus one vote in the film studios, the film distributors and the film production companies (*ibid.*: 13). In the financial sector, the state was to keep a 20 to 50 per cent interest in banks and insurance companies for the immediate future.

Pursuant to an Act that came into force on 28 August 1992, the State Asset Handling Company was established (AV Rt.). The purpose of the new company is to assume responsibility, in place of the SPA, over all assets to be retained by the State in the above-mentioned enterprises. An eleven-strong board of directors, whose members are nominated by the Privatization Minister and who are appointed by the Prime Minister, is in overall charge of the company.

## CONCLUSION

Privatization in Hungary has been characterized by the scale of its ambition and by the range, ingenuity and resourcefulness of the techniques employed. Nevertheless, despite these efforts, only 8.3 per cent of State-owned property was privatized in the two-and-a-half years following the formation of the SPA in March 1990 (*Figyelö*, 1 October 1992: 7). Moreover, many of the most commercially viable State-owned enterprises have already been sold to foreign investors, rendering the task of further privatization increasingly difficult.

Nevertheless, continued and accelerated privatization remains a central objective of the present administration. In a new privatization strategy, launched in September 1992 by Tamás Szabó, the minister responsible for privatization, privatization is seen as essential for Hungary's successful transition to a market economy. In particular, privatization is viewed as the key to creating a property-owning middle class, to attracting investment, to broadening the market in Hungary, to further structural reform and, increasingly, to creating a 'broad, strong, domestic owner class' (*Figyelö*, 1 October 1992: 7). The historic irony of this process, reversing the attempted elimination (literal as well as figurative) of the capitalist class in Hungary, must truly be savoured!

In a bid to increase the pace of privatization, most State-owned enterprises were required to draw up a 'transformation plan' by 30 June 1993, failing which the SPA would itself undertake their transformation into business organizations, a prerequisite for privatization (Ashton and Cohen, 1992: 25). More ominously, perhaps, plans are being drawn up for a 'privatization by voucher' scheme, similar to the Czech model. This would mark a considerable departure from Hungary's privatization strategy, which, at least until the privatization conception announced in September 1992, has emphasized the improved economic performance of enterprises as the fundamental goal of privatization, whether through the infusion of capital, or the acquisition of new technology or managerial skills. The current proposals would allow all Hungarian adults to acquire privatization vouchers in return for a registration fee (*Figyelö*, March 1993: 1). However, it is envisaged that such vouchers could only be used to obtain an interest in less commercially attractive enterprises and in concerns that have been excluded from the general privatization process. The more obviously successful enterprises would be privatized through established methods (*ibid.*). It has been suggested that the voucher scheme represents an attempt by an increasingly unpopular government, faced with the prospect of general elections in 1994, to restore its popularity with the electorate (*Financial Times*, 3 March 1993: 3).

## ACKNOWLEDGEMENT

I should like to acknowledge the generous support of the Nuffield Foundation, whose financial assistance enabled me to undertake the initial research for this Chapter in Hungary in September 1991. All translations from Hungarian-language texts are those of the author, unless specified to the contrary.

## BIBLIOGRAPHY

Ashton, K. and Cohen, R. (1992) 'Hungary'. In *International Financial Law Review*, Special Supplement, September, 24–6.

Bleaney, M. (1988) *Do Socialist Economies Work? The Soviet and East European Experience.* Oxford, Basil Blackwell.

Csillag, I. (1991) Magyarország, in Kálmán Mizsei. In *Privatizáció Kelet-Europában*, Atlantisz Kiadó, Budapest, Hungary.

*First Privatisation Programme 1990* (1990) State Property Agency, Budapest, Hungary.

Fricz, T. (1992) Partideológiák és Tagoltság. In Mihály Bihári (ed.), *A Tòbbpártrendszer Kialakulása Magyarországon 1985–1991.* Kossuth Könyvkiadó, Budapest, Hungary.

Matolcsy, Gy. (1991) *Labadozásunk Évei, A Magyar Privatizáció Trendek, Tények, Privatizácios Példák.* Privatizációs Kutatóintézet, Budapest, Hungary.

Pethö, R. and Jutasi, G. (1991) *Investors' Guide Manual for Investment in Hungary.* Vektori Kiadó, Budapest, Hungary.

Pogany, I. (1989) The regulation of foreign investment in Hungary, *ICSID Review – Foreign Investment Law Journal*, 4(1), 39–62.

Pogany, I. (1993) Constitutional reform in Central and Eastern Europe: Hungary's transition to democracy, *International and Comparative Law Quarterly*, 42(2), 332–55.

Sárközy, T. (1991) *A Privatizáció Joga Magyarországon.* UNIÓ Kft., Budapest, Hungary.

Sulkowski, H., Glick, S. and Richter, W. (1991) Privatisation in Hungary: the art of the possible, *International Financial Law Review*, April, 32–5.

Veljanovski, C. (1987) *Selling the State, Privatisation in Britain.* London, Weidenfeld and Nicolson.

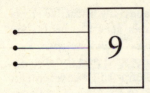

# THE POLITICAL ECONOMY OF ECOLOGICAL MODERNIZATION: CREATING A REGULATED MARKET FOR ENVIRONMENTAL QUALITY

## Kenneth Hanf

### MARKETS AND GOVERNMENT REGULATION

This chapter raises a number of crucial points regarding the extent to which a policy of privatization and deregulation alone can create an adequate framework and the preconditions for an effectively functioning market economy in the countries of Central Europe. It argues that the headlong rush to throw off the constraining shackles of the previous centrally planned and regulated system overlooks important insights into the legal or, perhaps in this context more correctly, the regulatory foundations of market capitalism.

Markets are not natural phenomena, emerging as finished products once economic decision-makers are released from the unnatural fetters of politically inspired bureaucratic regulations. The choice is not between a 'free' market and government regulation of the economy. Within some yet-to-be-determined limits, there is a range of market economies that will differ in their specific features depending upon the particular regulatory context defining the relation between market activity, on the one hand, and the set of overarching societal objectives that specify the limits under which this economic activity is to take place, on the other hand. Consequently, opting for a 'market economy' does not in itself answer the question as to the precise institutional form this economic order will take and the roles that will be played by the various public and private actors. Therefore, we must be wary of placing blind faith in measures designed to 'create a market' by laying control over the factors of productions in private hands.

Furthermore, there would seem to be at least three levels of institutional adaptation to market economies that should be distinguished. First of all, and predominant in most discussions of these problems, there is the need to create the conditions for a new macro-system based on relatively free play of market forces; this is the main focus for deregulation and privatization measures. In the second place, at an intermediate or meso level, an associational infrastructure must be created, either by adapting existing social and economic organizations or by creating new ones to perform various functions required by a capitalist economy. This will include redefining the working relation between government and the different economic actors. Third, the development of such a market system will require adjustments on the part of managers of industrial firms since managing a firm in a market situation is different from performing the same tasks in a planned economy in which the disciplining effects of market exchanges are absent. The same holds true for government officials whose job it has been to 'regulate' this economic activity in one way or another. The nature of the regulatory role of the State, the instruments employed and the relationships between regulatory agencies and their target groups will need to be adapted to the requirements of the institutional context of the particular market economy. These kinds of adjustments in the role conceptions and management skills of both public and private actors are important preconditions for the transition to an effectively working market order.

Creating market structures will involve, therefore, the development of a regulatory regime that will promote and, at the same time, socially 'discipline' market activities. In this sense, all market economies are mixed systems of governmental regulation and market forces. In short, markets are defined in terms of, and function within the boundaries set by, a particular politically determined regulatory space.[1] In order to understand the way in which a specific example of market economies operates it is necessary to understand the way in which the underlying regulatory framework defines the roles played by the various public and private actors involved, together with the relations among them, as well as the process by which the dimensions and structure of this space are negotiated – a dynamic process marked by consolidation and stability as well as renegotiation and restructuring.

These clarifications of the nature of market systems completed, we can now turn to the case of environmental regulation. We first take a brief look at how the notions of sustainable development and ecological modernization, which view the relationship between environmental quality and economic development in positive-sum terms, are being used in Western Europe to redefine the social context and overarching policy objectives for market-oriented economic activity. Against the background of these remarks, the succeeding sections of the chapter then examine developments around one case of the current redefinition of regulatory space in a particular West European country, the Netherlands. This discussion of the Dutch experience is intended to illustrate a number of recent general developments in Western Europe that are relevant to an evaluation of the policy of privatization and deregulation in Central Europe. Recent experiences with deregulation in the area of environmental policy, together with the debate in theory and practice within a number of Western European countries regarding the role and instruments of the post-war welfare state, are used to examine the way in which the balance has been struck between government intervention and reliance on the 'freer' play of market forces. In particular, the process by which a commitment to sustainable development has been leading to a restructuring of the regulatory space for a socially responsible market needs to be examined in the broader context of what might be called the 'recalibration of the welfare state.'

In country after country in Western Europe, both practical measures and theoretical discussion have been concerned with the question of the appropriate division of labour between State and society and, within the State itself, between the different levels of government authority. What can be seen here in the West – in many respects quite similar to the process underway in the East, although those countries are coming from another extreme – is the reinstitutionalization of relationships between key governmental and societal actors. From various quarters critics call for a general reconsideration for the need for government intervention in societal processes and, where this is considered necessary, for a re-examination of the types of instruments that can be used. Of particular importance is to make more use of the potential for self-regulation that an organized society contains. Between the extremes of a hierarchically organized system of bureaucratic governmental intervention and the free play of market forces there is, it is argued, an under-utilized societal capacity for self-organization and self-steering. No doubt, government will continue to fulfil a variety of indispensable regulative, facilitative and supporting functions. In particular, in those cases where it is not possible to leave things in the hands of the free interplay of these societal actors and where government intervention in the interest of the larger community interest is necessary, policy strategies and instruments will be required that take the emerging relation between government and society into account.

## SUSTAINABLE DEVELOPMENT: THE SOCIAL IMPERATIVE OF MARKET REGULATION

These general observations remind us that regulation is not an all-or-nothing phenomenon. Consequently, the way out of an overly regulated, regimented and planned economy into some form of a market economy does not necessarily require the denial of an active role for government, both in creating the institutional prerequisites for, and at the same time providing the societally determined normative constraints upon, the free play of these market forces. Together these regulatory actions define the particular political economy of the social market of a given country.

Economic regulation, broadly conceived, typically refers to governmental efforts to control the individual price, output or product quality decisions of private firms, in an avowed effort to prevent purely private decision-making that would take inadequate account of the 'public interest'. This public interest has to do, in the first instance, with preventing conditions from arising that would curb or undermine market competition itself – in this sense government intervenes to protect the market against abuses of concentration, unfair competition, etc. In addition, the public interest takes the form of certain social values that would not otherwise be protected or promoted by market forces and economic exchanges alone. Such things as worker health and safety, consumer protection and environmental quality have formed the basis for such social regulation.

In the past, the design of environmentally compatible manufacturing plants has generally entailed the use of end-of-pipe treatment techniques (those various devices through which effluent gases or liquid pass on the way to the environment). The past few years have seen a shift of emphasis in this regard toward in-plant practices (as opposed to add-on devices or exterior recycling) to reduce or eliminate waste. Here the focus is on waste reduction or pollution prevention. Whereas control at the source is intended to prevent emissions into the environment in the first place, more traditional abatement control has been designed to render emissions harmless to the environment. In this sense, many people are speaking of a fundamental paradigm shift regarding the way in which we deal with pollution problems. Insofar as environmental policy takes these imperatives seriously, there will be important consequences for both industry and government. Crucial in this connection will be determining the extent to which government regulation can actively promote and support these efforts to achieve preventive, waste-reduction policies within industrial firms and the measures through which this can be achieved. In particular, preventing pollution will require changing policies of governments and business institutions so as to encourage the adoption of clean technologies and products by individual firms.

With respect to the economic transition under way in the countries of Central Europe two inter-related processes have to be examined. On the one hand, economic activity is being released from the confines of the socialist economic system and exposed to the dynamic forces of the market. But, at the same time, this emerging market system is subject to new constraints intended to ensure that economic activity also respects and promotes certain overarching social values not necessarily protected by market-driven economic decision-making. What is happening then is a general restructuring of the previously centrally planned economy by creating preconditions for a socially regulated market economy. This is clearly no simple move from a very heavily (centrally, bureaucratically) regulated economy to a completely unregulated economy (where privatization and deregulation are guiding principles). The regulative principle here is the search for an appropriate balance between governmental intervention and the free play of market forces to promote a process of ecological modernization in support of the objectives of a sustainable societal development.

The notion of sustainable development, together with ecological modernization, promises policy-makers a win-win situation in which the objectives of economic development and environmental quality both presuppose and reinforce each other. In this sense, preventive environmental policy becomes a fundamental precondition for effective economic reform and long-term development. At the same time, it is one of the societal constraints that defines what kind of economic activity will be permitted. Phrased in normative terms this means that if the goal of sustainable development is taken seriously, economic reform and market activity cannot be allowed to threaten or to ignore environmental policy objectives. The restructuring of these economies must be carried out in such a way as to both contribute a cleaning up of damage from the socialist system and lead to integrated preventive strategies as central elements of strategic and operational planning at all levels of action, from the formulation of governmental policy down to the operational management of firms.

The normative orientation for the new social market is to be provided by the goal of ecological modernization as both the basis for and an expression of integration of economic development and environmental quality policy objectives. But why should this goal of sustainable development be taken seriously as a regulatory principle by policy-makers in Central European countries? While it seems to offer the philosopher's stone for avoiding politically unpleasant trade-offs between economic growth and environmental quality, it would seem that these countries have other, more pressing priorities. Are they not, understandably, more concerned with achieving a rapid improvement of their countries' standard of living by allowing as much room as is possible for the free play of market forces? Is not economic development the most pressing concern in order to curb social unrest and promote political stability? Is not environmental protection a luxury for which these countries cannot avoid to pay the economic price?

There are at least three ways by which a political commitment to the strategy of sustainable development could come about. First of all, the politically relevant groups in these societies could demand it, with or without the support of the main economic actors. Or the political leadership itself might become sold on the idea and attempt to convince the relevant domestic actors of the need to integrate both the environmental preconditions and consequences of economic activity into the country's development strategy. Equally possible is that this commitment could be imposed upon the policy-makers by the relevant actor-system outside the country, i.e. the European Community, as the price for participation in the broader system of European economic co-operation. For the moment it is this latter source of pressure, in the form of the different association agreements with the EC, that is an important factor shaping domestic policy decisions. In turn, this EC pressure works either to reinforce already-present indigenous forces or to stimulate them to emerge to support EC demands.

A similar combination of domestic and international pressures for sustainable development is also at work in Western European countries. In the following sections of this chapter we examine the impact that such an attempt to pursue sustainable development paths has had for relations between State and economy. More specifically, we will draw on experience in the Netherlands with deregulation in the area of environmental policy to argue that this restructuring of regulatory space has involved the creation of the preconditions for (a particular kind of) self-regulation (as an integral part of a larger system of government regulation with regard to environmentally relevant activities).

It is argued here that Central European countries do not really have the choice of a completely deregulated and privatized market economy. The transformation of their economies will also require that they confront the need to integrate economic development and environmental quality. They, too, will be forced to regulate their market economy on the basis of some kind of commitment – enforced or freely chosen – to sustainable development through the ecological modernization of the economy. Of course, the fact that similar developments can be discerned in these various countries does not mean that events in Central Europe will follow the same path as in the Netherlands, or that of other West European countries. Ecological modernization defines a certain overall balance between government intervention and market forces; it involves a particular structuring of regulatory space with regard to environmental quality objectives. But it comes in many shapes and sizes, and the bottom line results are not guaranteed by a policy commitment to this strategy alone. Those details will also be provided by the interplay of domestic and international political forces. The Dutch example can, nevertheless, suggest some of the ways in which the emerging combination of external and emerging internal pressures for an environmentally-sensitive (constrained) economic development might shape the political economy of these countries.

## BEYOND DEREGULATION: THE CASE OF THE NETHERLANDS

In the eyes of many critics, environmental policy measures have contributed greatly to the regulatory costs borne by economic actors in Western European countries. Even though available evidence suggests that the actual burden of these regulations has been neither as heavy as critics would have us believe nor even as severe as they could have been based on the formal possibilities of the measures themselves,[2] environmental regulatory programmes have been one of the prime targets of attack for those who seek to limit governmental intervention in economic affairs.

In the Netherlands a primary stimulus for deregulation was the perceived crisis of the welfare state and the economic system on which it has rested.[3] As part of the political response to these problems, deregulation measures were originally intended as a means for radically reducing the scope of government, in general, and for cutting back much of its regulatory activity, in particular. In this respect, deregulation formed an integral part of a search for an answer to the problems plaguing the intervention state. It was intended to constitute a central element of the process by which what government was doing and how it went about its business was to be reconsidered.

The move to deregulate must also be seen in the context of a stagnating economy and the resulting financial difficulties of government. A main cause of economic slowdown was seen in the fact that the plethora of governmental regulations and controls discouraged necessary investments. The political career of the Dutch deregulation operation was given an accelerating push by the sudden attention to supply-side economics in the early 1980s. The arguments of this school of thought found a receptive ear in the liberal-conservative government of that time. (Over)regulation, it was argued, had led to unacceptable financial burdens for citizens and firms with serious consequences for the functioning of the market. Deregulation would improve the climate for investment and economic development by re-establishing the market as the chief mechanism for guiding and rewarding entrepreneurial activities.

The combination of political pressure from the business community and the growing problems encountered in financing and managing various interventionist programmes of the welfare state convinced government that economic recovery, on which these same public expenditures ultimately depended, could only be achieved by restoring the disciplining effect of the profit margin and, in this way, encouraging new investments. This, in turn, presupposed the removal of all kinds of obstacles perceived as hindering business activity. It was in this connection that the reduction of government controls and simplification of remaining procedures was expected to contribute to the expansion of employment as a result of general economic growth resulting from the more favourable conditions for investment and production.

However, the mitigation of the negative effects of environmental regulations for business was not to be realized by lowering the level of effective protection of the quality of the environment. Deregulation was not to be pursued as an end in itself but rather constituted a critical re-examination of the means by which established policy goals were to be sought. A careful policy of deregulation, operating within the parameters of prevailing quality objectives, was to reduce the burden of industry while, at the same time, improving the possibilities of achieving intended objectives. In this sense, a primary goal of the regulatory reforms introduced with the package of 'deregulation measures' for this policy field was the improvement of the quality of the instruments of environmental management and an increase in the effectiveness and efficiency of the regulatory system as a whole.

Whatever the original policy objectives of the Dutch Cabinet, in this particular policy area deregulation thus took on the guise of regulatory reform. Here deregulation did not mean the dismantling of the substantive regulations designed to promote improved environmental quality. When all is said and done, the bottom line of the deregulation efforts with regard to environmental management has been the retention, essentially intact, of the overall regulatory objectives while striving to simplify and streamline existing regulatory procedures and to develop alternatives to the more traditional instruments of regulation. As such, deregulation in this area is a good example of a variation of the theme of 're-regulation', i.e. steps taken to make existing regulations more effective or to replace rules with other instruments designed to achieve more effectively and efficiently the same behavioural changes sought with the original regulatory scheme.

Viewed in this way, as part of a continuing effort to improve the performance of the system of environmental management, deregulation can be understood as an acknowledgement that with time regulations can lose their initial meaning (and, indeed, under changed conditions, become counterproductive) not only in terms of their own objectives, but also in relation to other, often competing, social values. Furthermore, shifts in societal priorities can affect the relative balance of the costs and benefits on which the original policy strategy had been based. If, however, there continues to be a politically expressed societal interest in steering these activities (i.e. the environmentally relevant behaviours of economic decision-makers) in a particular direction, new regulations must be promulgated or more efficient, alternative means of reaching the same objectives must be found.

Deregulation continues to occupy an important place on the government's agenda as a general guiding consideration, in principle if not in name. The government's deregulation vision emphasizes the need to keep government at an arm's length from the citizen and economic activity, and to promote various forms of privatization, i.e. giving back to society the primary responsibility for governing the relations among citizens. It is the view of the Dutch government that any form of government regulation (i.e. intervention in societal affairs by means of formal legal acts) is excessive if it is possible to leave things to the responsibility of the affected societal actors themselves. Thus if firms can handle their own affairs, assisted by professional or sectoral interest organizations and mutual agreements, then there is no need (indeed no legitimation) for public law regulation of these affairs.

For the Dutch government, systematic concern for the environment at the level of the individual industrial enterprise must be an integral part of its overall system for managing environmental quality. The role of such self-responsibility on the part of firms for policy enforcement not only fits nicely with the idea of deregulation, but also follows from one of the central implications of the preventive policy strategy on which sustainable development ultimately depends: effective environmental policy must build on the motivations and world of experience of those whose behaviour is to be modified. By means of a supportive and stimulating policy the government is presently attempting to contribute to the effective institutionalization of such a capacity. The objective of this policy is to make Dutch firms themselves responsible (up to a certain point) for the enforcement of the regulations applying to them.

## SOFT REGULATION AND THE REDEFINITION OF THE RELATION BETWEEN STATE AND SOCIETY

In most countries, the initial policy response to emerging environmental problems was based on familiar direct regulation: environmentally friendly action was to be promoted or activities detrimental to the environment were to be prevented by means of rules and regulations forbidding certain kinds of behaviours or by stipulating the conditions under which they would be permitted. Now that environmental values appear to be more deeply anchored in society and environmental policy itself is better developed, it is being argued that other instruments are more appropriate for influencing behaviour in the desired direction. For example, economists in particular have long set great store by some form of economic incentives or market-like mechanisms to encourage firms to behave in an environmentally responsible manner.

As we have noted, in the case of the Netherlands, in addition to instruments of direct and indirect regulation, there has been a growing interest in the possibilities of stimulating the internalization of responsibility for the environmental consequences of their actions by the target groups themselves as a basis for some form of self-regulation.

When viewed as regulatory reform, deregulation can be interpreted as an attempt to influence the behaviour of environmentally relevant actors in a more effective and, particularly, more efficient way. In the first instance, this means that instruments are to be used that inhibit as little as possible the 'market efficient behaviour' of the firms or economic actors involved. Government will still intervene in private decision-making by setting constraints upon the decisional autonomy of the actors or defining the parameters for a general range of acceptable action alternatives. However, this is to be done in such a way that quality objectives sought can be realized while at the same time the 'freedom' or leeway of the firm to respond to market developments is enhanced.

As Majone has noted, the rationale for public intervention has seldom been challenged in the increasingly important area of 'social' regulation (Majone, 1990: 3). In a similar vein, Breyer has pointed out that

> The deregulation movement has found it more difficult to achieve significant change in classical regulatory programmes governing health, safety and the environment, areas where the economic rationale for government interventions is stronger, and the free market alternatives to classical regulation less obviously superior.
>
> (1990: 17)

In these areas, he continues, 'regulatory reform pressure has taken the form of advocating, not total deregulation, but rather less restrictive or less burdensome methods of governmental interventions aimed at achieving the relevant regulatory end' (*ibid.*: 17).

Along with the measures taken to improve the efficiency of regulatory instruments there has also been increasing interest in developing alternative instruments, which are to be used together with or in place of direct regulation, for stimulating the responsibility of the target groups themselves for measures to promote environmental quality. Encouraging self-responsibility on the part of the target groups is a relatively new element in Dutch environmental policy. The point of departure in this connection is the assumption that the success of the government's 'source oriented' policy strategy will ultimately depend on abatement and other preventive measures being taken by the target firms themselves on the basis of their own concern for the quality of the environment. In the long run, it is argued, the quality of the environment will as a whole be determined by the willingness of those whose activities are being regulated to change their behaviour with regard to the environment. In this connection it is crucial that industrial enterprises, on the basis of their awareness of their own responsibility in this area, make the environment an integral part of the daily operations of the firm. The more government measures are consistent with the world of experience and possibilities of the target group, the greater will be the chance that cost effective and practicable solutions can be developed.

Again, it is not a question of regulation or no regulation but rather one of finding the appropriate kinds of governmental interventions – intended to shape and steer economic activity in socially desirable (as defined through the political process) ways. This will mean that traditional forms of direct intervention will be replaced or supplemented by various modes of more indirect guidance. And this in turn means replacing the 'hard' instruments of direct regulation with the 'soft' intervention modes of indirect and self-regulation. In any case it is important to keep in mind the need for various governmental initiatives – jointly conceived with target groups – to stimulate and encourage, but also to 'keep socially honest' the market-oriented decision-making of economic actors.

This is all a part of the process of redefining the relations between society and its governmental authorities and the working out of a new division of labour and pattern of collaboration between them. Students of alternative regulatory schemes for promoting new environmental protection strategies stress that efforts to prevent pollution will need to become a joint responsibility – in an important sense, a co-produced result. The character of the regulatory relation between business and government will need to shift from confrontation to collaboration. At the heart of their vision is the belief that socially responsible self-interest can be mobilized in support of long-term adjustments towards pollution prevention. Supporting this faith is the already visible growing awareness on the part of some large corporations that continued corporate existence depends on the environmental performance of the firms and enterprise and the continued support of public and government.

One important question remains: What is the most appropriate strategy for ensuring that firms proceed to set up effective systems of environmental management by incorporating their environmental responsibility into the strategic planning, organization, and operations of the enterprise? For the moment, the Netherlands has opted for a voluntary approach. A government White Paper outlining the policy on this matter, states what is expected of the business community, by when and with what assistance from the government itself (Ministry of Environment, 1989). Not surprisingly, many doubt that much can be achieved on the basis of the voluntary actions of business alone. There are, for example, those who argue that 'business is just as likely to proceed, on large scale, to introduce internal environmental management on a voluntary basis as turkeys are to vote for an early Christmas!' (Van Kleef, 1991: 4). According to these critics, only an effective 'regulatory stick' behind the door, and the will to wield it, will motivate firms to change their ways.

But things may not be quite as simple as that. Firms themselves also have a number of reasons for being interested in promoting a system of self-regulation. To begin with, they share the deepening societal commitment to the values of environmental concern. It is too simplistic to picture industry as a bunch of bad ogres out to exploit the natural environment while denying any responsibility for the impact of their actions on environmental quality. Still, even well-meaning, environmentally committed firms need to keep their concern for environmental quality in proper perspective: competing demands on limited resources and the economic health of the enterprise both set limits to what a firm can 'afford' to do for environmental management. Of course, by agreeing to forms of self-regulation, industry hopes to keep the government at arm's length and to avoid more intrusive intervention into the internal workings of the firm. This, it is assumed, will lead to lower regulatory burdens by reducing costs associated with tighter administrative controls but also (and more importantly) will leave firms more leeway to be guided by market considerations when deciding how they can most efficiently meet given quality objectives.

## CO-OPERATIVE SELF-REGULATION: CREATING A MARKET FOR ENVIRONMENTAL QUALITY

The experience with deregulation in the Netherlands and elsewhere suggests that as long as the regulatory impulse (i.e. the policy commitment to the general objective of environmental quality) persists, deregulation measures will result primarily in adjustments – in the interest of a more efficient and effective pursuit of the objectives of environmental policy – within the general framework of the existing system of regulation. Such re-regulation defines a new mode of intervention into private decision-making by which government continues to attempt to influence the behaviour of environmentally relevant actors. A new mix of regulatory instruments is to ensure that this intervention is carried out in a more effective and efficient manner, by tapping into the capacity of the affected societal actors for a significant amount of self-regulation.

Deregulation in the Netherlands has then not involved the abolition of, or even a fundamental alteration in the basic set of, regulatory constraints on economic activity through which the country's commitment to environmental quality has been defined. Nor has it brought about any significant changes in the mechanisms that hold the existing system of environmental regulation in place; the system of regulatory co-production[4] continues to be the basis of the Dutch system of co-operative environmental management, albeit complemented with newer instruments, of social regulation. The underlying regulatory impulse carrying these environmental policy measures remains operative and, therefore, continues to legitimate and give direction to regulatory intervention shaping market behaviour in an environmentally friendly manner.

Deregulation has, nevertheless, involved a certain renegotiation of the terms of agreement defining the rules of the game between government and economic actors with regard to the general objectives to be pursued and the apportioning of the relative burdens to be borne by the individual firms in the different sectors of the economy in meeting these goals. In particular, a central role in this emerging regulatory system has been given to the institutionalization by the firms of their responsibility for the environmental impact of their activities. This capacity for preventative policy and self-control is a fundamental precondition for self-regulation on the part of target groups themselves within the general regulatory framework set by governmental policy. Once in place, systems of environmental management within individual firms will enable government authorities to redefine the manner in which they perform their traditional regulatory tasks at the interface with members of the business community. Moreover, a series of consultative bodies and negotiating arenas have been set up to provide an overarching structure within which the different levels of government and organized representatives of the target groups jointly work out the programmatic measures through which general policy objectives are translated into specific reduction targets and the means for realizing them.

In this way, deregulation in the Netherlands in the area of environmental policy has resulted in a restructuring of regulatory space by creating the preconditions for a particular kind of self-regulation as an integral part of a larger system of government regulation of environmentally-relevant activities. What we see in this policy area is a redefinition of the traditional regulatory relationship between government and the economy to create something that could be called 'co-operative self-regulation.' This involves, on one hand, the freeing up of certain kinds of restraints so as to expose economic actors to the discipline of market; and on the other hand, creating a market for environmental quality to which these actors can respond when making product and investment decisions.

Co-operative self-regulation differs in significant ways from earlier arrangements where an area of economic activity was allowed to establish and police the rules governing the behaviour of its members within a closed regulatory community shielded from the attention of democratic politics; where members of the profession or industry in question could manage their own affairs with or without support from government actors, so as to preclude more direct and restrictive intervention by public authority. In contrast to such schemes of self-regulation, government is now no longer an exogenous (threatening) factor outside the co-operative regulatory arrangement. On the contrary, government actors are actively involved in (co-) defining rules as well as policing or controlling the behaviour of other participants.

Thus, in the last analysis, regulatory reform has been designed to provide increasing leeway for economic actors (deregulation) in order to improve their ability to respond to market signals and developments while at the same time ensuring that they will take responsibility for the development of pollution prevention strategies within the parameters set by the government's environmental policy objectives (re-regulation). Such a system of co-operative self-regulation not only provides economic actors with substantial leeway in deciding themselves how they will meet these quality objectives, but also guarantees them an active role in co-determining what the general policy goals will mean for particular industrial branches and, ultimately, the individual firms. Both policy making and more specific rule making become processes of joint decision-making based on extensive consultation and bargaining between government and the affected target groups of governmental intervention.

The renegotiation of the agreements governing the relations between government and economic actors has resulted in the restructuring of regulatory space around a point of equilibrium between concern for environmental quality on the part of economic actors and improved economic competitiveness of firms as a result of increased responsiveness to market forces. Both in response to political pressures from voters and action groups – forces at work in the traditional political market – and as a result of direct consultation and bargaining between government and representatives of economic sector(s) a regulatory framework has been created that in turn generates the market forces that are to be relied upon to discipline the decision calculations of individual economic actors.

In order to understand how government intervention has worked to create such a regulated market for environmental quality, the following points should be kept in mind. At the ideological or programmatic level deregulation has been carried by the call to unshackle business from bureaucratic regulations and free it to respond to market forces. To the extent that society wishes to promote certain collective environmental quality objectives, it should be left to the firms themselves to decide in what ways their activities can be brought into conformity with these objectives by allowing them to respond to the same kinds of market considerations that guide their decisions on investment and production. However, there is an important difference between deregulation in the area of economic regulation and deregulation with regard to social regulation. It is difficult to imagine what would it mean to determine environmental quality decisions on the basis of the free play of 'market forces'. The original problem giving rise to government intervention in the first place was – and remains – that the market alone can not deal adequately with the problem of the negative externalities of production that we experience as pollution. Consequently, there are no market forces to rely on or to return to, once regulations have been lifted, to promote the politically defined objectives of socially acceptable environmental conditions.

On the other hand, as we have seen, deregulation is less about leaving environmental quality at the mercy of free market forces and more about the relation between the instruments to be used in pursuing these objectives and the impact of these policy constraints on the ability of the affected firm to act efficiently in the market-place. Government intervention in private decision-making to correct shortcomings of the market is not to be abolished by deregulation. Public authority is still to be used to influence economic behaviour in an environmentally friendly direction. What is to be changed, within these continuing policy parameters, is the mix of instruments through which these behaviours are to be affected. Both by rationalizing the instrumentalities of direct regulation and by making greater use of economic incentives as well as by institutionalizing self-responsibility into the daily operations of the firm (self-regulation), more leeway is to be given to the firm to select its own response to the constraints of environmental regulation in making its firm-specific market calculations. By simultaneously retaining the objectives of environmental regulation and increasing the firm's ability to adapt to the market, it is assumed that the goals of economic development and a socially-efficient environmental protection can be achieved together.

All well and good, as long as we keep in mind that government regulation continues to be the basis on which the effectiveness of these alternative instruments of environmental policy depends. Consequently, if 'care of the environment' is to become good business practice, there will have to be some kind of economic bottom-line conditions or incentives to stimulate and carry this commitment. It would, clearly, be unrealistic to expect industrial managers to take actions that undermine or are at odds with the well-understood economic interests of their firm. Their commitment to environmental responsibility needs to be carried by its consistency with market logic. At the same time, however, if the fundamental economic cause of environmental pollution is the failure of the market (under normal conditions) to provide the signals that would force economic decision-makers to internalize all the relevant costs of production / consumption, then these 'signals' (prices) have to be introduced by government (external) action.

In this important sense, then, it is the regulatory activity of government (in response to the politically articulated will of the community) that creates the market situation in terms of which firms calculate the cost/benefit ratios of responses to economic incentives for environmentally sound behaviour or to the atttractiveness of governmental initiatives on pollution prevention. While industrial managers may indeed be moved by notions of moral responsibility and personal feelings regarding environmental quality, they will, in the last analysis, act on the basis of economic rationality. If pollution prevention is to pay (i.e. be in the long-term economic interest of firms in the broadest sense, not just in terms of short-term, immediate profit), government policy must help structure the market so that it provides appropriate signals for calculating these pay offs.

Co-operative self-regulation within such a regulated market for environmental quality has also led to the enlargement of the community of relevant actors involved both in negotiating the regulatory agreements and in the functioning of the markets these measures create. A number of actors in addition to national government participate in the translation of general objectives into operative goals and procedures. These include representatives from sub-national governmental authorities, the target groups themselves, and other interested groups in society. Once in place, the market creates both new opportunities and risks, which, in turn, mobilize new and old actors. For example, legislation defining the legal liability of firms for environmental pollution affects the market for liability insurance. This then leads insurance companies to evaluate a particular company's risk, and thus the premium it must pay, in terms of the in-house capacity of the firm to manage its environmental affairs effectively. Likewise, the loan and investment policies of financial institutions, including banks and financial markets, can be geared to the perceived 'greenness' of the firm in question. And of course, government programmes regarding product information and labelling reinforce the position of consumers demanding environmentally friendly products. In this way, then, private market actors perform important functions within the overall system of public regulation.

These, then, are some of the ways in which government policy creates the foundation on which this particular social market economy is based and also generates the incentives (both positive and negative) that ensure that economic actors will remain sensitive to the market forces so created. This combination of market incentives and regulatory constraints provides the material basis for a system of self-regulation that is not just a question of good will and admirable intentions. Co-operative self-regulation requires the discipline of both a publicly-structured market and the ultimate threat of the regulatory stick to keep things honest.

## THE POLITICAL ECONOMY OF MARKET CREATION

This chapter has attempted to make two general points, intended to qualify the enthusiasm for privatization and deregulation as the primary tools for transforming Central European economic systems into functioning market economies. First, we have argued that all market economies are in a fundamental sense regulated economies. Given the external and, in the long run, internal (domestic) pressure for sustainable development, the socially regulated market economy will have as one important limiting factor (upon the free play of market forces) the commitment to a strategy of ecological modernization as a central element of its policy for environmental quality. In Western countries, this commitment has involved a reordering of regulatory space in a search for a balance between market forces and government regulation of a new type. By creating the kind of regulated market described above, the objectives of sustainable development are to be achieved by introducing considerations of environmental quality and care as parameters for the decisions of economic actors.

Second, a market is not just the sum total of freely deciding producers and equally autonomous consumers seeking the best bargain; markets of all kinds require the creation of a variety of institutions to carry the activities. The transformation of an economic system requires, therefore, not only the regulatory underpinnings supplied by governmental policy, but also the necessary organizational infrastructure, either by establishing new institutions or adapting old ones to the various functions that must be performed if a market is to operate efficiently. It is clear, for example, that if a central element of co-operative self-regulation involves consultation and bargaining between government and target groups, then there must be an intermediary organization to represent those segments of society. A strategy of ecological modernization based on co-operative self-regulation requires a wide range of organizational actors, within both government and society. In this sense a regulated market for environmental quality also rests upon the associational life of society as a whole.

What this all means is that the creation of a market economy committed to ecological modernization requires more than just the transfer of ownership of assets to private hands and the discarding of regulations that restrict the decision-making freedom of market-oriented actors. The challenge faced in economic change in Central Europe goes beyond the privatization and deregulation of what has been inherited. If all markets are organized or, in an important sense, publicly regulated, then the preconditions for the transition from centrally planned economies to some form of market economy also include the organizational underpinnings on which the effective functioning of such an economic system ultimately depends.

This is perhaps the greatest challenge faced by the countries of Central

Europe in transforming their economies: creating the institutional capacities required to put into place and to operate the kind of system of socially responsible self-regulation that is an integral part of a market for sustainable development. This new kind of regulatory capacity (in the service of preventive environmental policy) places especially great demands on the capabilities of sub-national governmental authorities. It will also require new habits of mind and management skills at the level of the individual firms. Moreover, both government and industry will need the assistance of a number of supporting actors in redefining the appropriate relationships between the private and the public in the new economy.

The Dutch experience with deregulation and the search for alternative means of pursuing environmental quality objectives has underscored the fact that governmental regulation is not an all or nothing matter. Deregulation does not necessarily mean dismantling all the rules and regulations placed by public authority (in the name of some set of social objectives) upon the market. The political economy of sustainable development is based on policy measures putting in place the regulatory regime by means of which the market incorporates the incentives necessary to encourage ecological modernization. It creates a situation where, on the one hand, government intervenes to increase and support market-oriented behaviour while, on the other hand, policy intervenes to promote values not produced by unregulated market forces. An analysis of the political economy of this transformation process focuses attention on the role that government must play in defining the regulatory structure of the new economic system. It also makes us aware of the way in which this restructuring of regulatory space also mobilizes a variety of actors and provides incentives to tie their material interests to the promotion of environmental quality objectives. But such an analysis also needs to examine the way in which the need continually to redress the balance between economic development and environmental protection generates a political process through which actors and interest compete in the political market-place to define the conditions under which economic activity will be carried out.

## NOTES

1  On the concept of 'regulatory space' see Hancher and Moran (1989).
2  For a discussion of the difference between predicted and actual compliance costs see Peacock (1984).
3  The description presented here of the inception of the Dutch deregulation programme is based on Hanf (1989).
4  See Hanf (1993) for an analysis of co-production in connection with regulatory policy.

BIBLIOGRAPHY

Breyer, S. (1990) Regulation and deregulation in the United States: Airlines, telecommunications and antitrust. In G. Majone (ed) *Deregulation or Re-regulation? Regulatory Reform in Europe and the United States*, London, Pinter Publishers.

Hanf, K. (1989) Deregulation as regulatory reform: the case of environmental policy in the Netherlands, *European Journal of Political Research*, 17, 193–207.

Hanf, K. (1993) Enforcing environmental laws. The social regulation of co-production. In M. Hill (ed.) *New Agendas in the Study of the Policy Process*. Brighton, Harvester Wheatsheaf.

Hancher L. and Moran, M. (1989) Organizing regulatory space. In L. Hancher and M. Moran (eds) *Capitalism, Culture and Economic Regulation*. Oxford. Clarendon Press.

van Kleef, M. (1991) Grote voordelen door integration (Great advantages from integration), *Milieumagazine*, 2, 4–7.

Majone, G. (1990) Introduction. In G. Majone (ed.) *Deregulation or Re-regulation? Regulatory Reform in Europe and the United States*. London, Pinter Publishers.

Ministry of Environment (1989) Notitie Bedrijfsinterne Milieuzorg (Memorandum on Environmental Management with the Firm), Second Chamber, Session 1988–9, 20 633, nr.2.

Peacock, A. (1989) *The Regulation Game. How British and West German Companies Bargain with Government*. Oxford, Basil Blackwell.

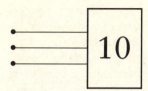

**10**

# CONCLUSION: FROM NATIONAL UNIQUENESS TO SUPRA-NATIONAL CONSTITUTION

## Tony Prosser and Michael Moran

The organization of the chapters in this book betrays an assumption that has guided much of the enterprise. Most of the contributors address, because they were asked to address, particular national experiences. That bias reflects the assumption that, in understanding the experience of economic change, nations matter: in other words, the territory where change is experienced is itself an important influence in shaping the form taken by the changes in question. In a world where the most important economic enterprises are organized on a multinational scale, and where markets are increasingly global in reach, this may seem an odd assumption. Indeed, one way of making sense of the momentous economic changes now taking place in Eastern Europe is to see them as completing the process by which the distinct economic system of Eastern Europe created by Soviet hegemony is being incorporated into the mainstream of the international capitalist economy.

### NATIONAL UNIQUENESS

Nevertheless, a stress on national uniqueness as a key influence on the nature of privatization and the style of regulation has found ample justification in these pages. National setting matters for three overwhelmingly important reasons. The first is a contingency of history. During the period when this volume was being assembled one of the cases – Czechoslovakia – disappeared in its old form. Its disappearance was obviously one manifestation – a civilized manifestation compared with signs elsewhere in the old Soviet sphere of influence – of the resurgence of national sentiment in politics. Nationalism has revived as perhaps the most potent political force in Eastern Europe; and as in the Czechoslovak case, nationalist sentiments have shaped responses to the challenges of economic change. Any account of the attempt to marketize the old command economies that ignored the nationalist context would be seriously incomplete.

The second important reason for the continuing relevance of the national setting has reappeared time and again in this volume: the starting point from which national economic systems approach the experiments of privatization and deregulation are unique, and this has produced major divergencies in the nature of the privatization process. For example, Britain, Germany and Italy all emerge with different configurations of interests, different institutional structures and different constitutional traditions. In Britain the major theme has been a programme of privatization; deregulation has played a secondary role, and where it has been necessary to re-regulate this has proceeded in a highly pragmatic fashion. By contrast, in Germany until recently deregulation played a more important role than did privatization, especially in labour markets but also in other areas such as financial services, though this seems largely to have been as a result of pressures from the European Community. In Italy, the peculiarly opaque nature of the regulatory state has meant that there has been little deregulation; although a considerable number of individual privatizations have been achieved, the strong resistance of the Italian political system to policy implementation has made it exceedingly difficult for successive governments to implement a privatization programme. In this respect the resistance of the system even where financial pressures would seem to make a disposal of public enterprises a matter of urgency places Italy at the opposite extreme to Britain.

Our lesson here, then, is that there is no typical 'capitalist' economy, and this is true even in the implementation of policies with similar economic and financial rationales. We are also now learning that there was no 'typical' command economy; the legacies faced by Poland, Hungary and the former Czechoslovakia, as described in these pages, are strikingly different and have led to the adoption of very different solutions to their problems. For example, in Hungary the greater degree of marketization even before the fall of the Communist regime has been one influence in enabling an approach to be taken that stresses the role of market sales as a discipline in the privatization process, rather than adopting free distribution through vouchers or large-scale restitution. In the former Czechoslovakia, however, the particularly high degree of State dominance of the economy up to the arrival of the new regime and the shortage of domestic capital has led to the adoption of a voucher scheme for large-scale privatization, which in turn has created problems owing to the role of initially unregulated investment funds whose extravagant promises threatened the whole future of the programme. In Poland, National Investment Funds have been created as part of the privatization process itself.

The privatization process has thus been conducted differently to reflect differing national characteristics. It is worth noting also that the actors in the programme have also varied to reflect the differing political and constitutional systems. Thus in Hungary the Constitutional Court has played a key role in permitting the privatization programme to take place by offering a definition of property rights that facilitated the process; as we stressed in the chapter on Britain, the near-total absence of any controversy over property ownership significantly assisted the implementation of the British programme. In Germany, the role of the Constitutional Court has now gained importance with the extension of privatization to enterprises given a protected constitutional status. In Italy, the complex webs created through patronage and based on the political parties have also played a role in making the implementation of a privatization programme more difficult.

This leads to our final reason for the importance of the national setting; that of regulatory styles. Nothing in this volume has suggested that privatization is somehow an alternative to regulation; rather the necessity of regulation runs through all the contributions. This can apply to the process of privatization itself; apart from the problem already mentioned of the unregulated investment funds in the former Czechoslovakia, we have also had demonstrated the role of the Antimonopoly Office in Poland and the need in Hungary to establish the State Property Agency to counter the dangers of 'spontaneous privatization'. Indeed, perhaps paradoxically, the problems experienced in implementing the Italian privatization programme can be partially attributed to the absence of a strong centralized force able to supervise such implementation.

A further regulatory issue is that of regulation after privatization. The question of national regulatory styles was, of course, explored in Vogel's (1986) landmark study. Regardless of the rise of nationalism, or of the institutional structures and interest patterns developed in different nations, ways of going about the practice of regulation remain stubbornly individual in different national jurisdictions. It is impossible to read Markowski's account of the reconstruction of the system of environmental regulation in Poland as separable from the national setting in which it is being attempted; indeed, it raises further, complex, yet crucially important, questions of the degree to which legal styles and the form of legal instruments can be changed in the sort of rapid transformation required in the transition from Communism. His stress on the post-Communist attitude to law as an instrumental tool of the State that can be easily evaded or ignored hardly bodes well for an effective system of environmental regulation.

The current alternative to an instrumental regulation through formal legal devices is, of course, self-regulation; yet it is also clear from these pages that this portmanteau term can cover a variety of institutional forms. In the context of environmental regulation, Hanf in his contribution describes limitations to this regulatory form and underlines its role in supplementing rather than supplanting other controls. Whatever the general attractions of self-regulation, more work needs to be done on its cultural preconditions; these must include a degree of stability that is highly unlikely to obtain in the rapid changes characteristic of the Central European experience described here.

We would stress, then, that nation and territory matter in the process of privatization and regulatory change. However, on the other hand, the emergence of the European Community as a major actor in processes of economic change is heralding the creation of a supranational constitutional context to challenge this national context. In the rest of this chapter we shall chart the novelty of the developing supranational constitution.

## THE SUPRANATIONAL CONSTITUTION

One of our dominant themes, then, has been the importance of national characteristics in shaping the regulatory policy that is an inevitable requirement of privatization. However, there are signs that in some important respects the key role of national uniqueness is ending. It is now a truism to remark that legal and policy-making processes are strongly shaped by the institutions of the European Community, and we would make the further claim that, even in Great Britain, the constitutional elements we found lacking in relation to British privatization are to be found in Community law; in this sense the Community treaties can be seen as forming a sort of constitution for economic life. The argument that the Community has powerful constitutional effects is of course familiar: consider the incorporation of certain human rights into the Community law framework, and the development of concepts such as proportionality. But the effect goes much deeper: either actually or potentially each of the aspects of privatization identified above on which the British government was unconstrained by domestic law are areas on which an emerging Community constitutional structure can be found.

To this we can add two further points. First, constitutional effects exist independently of the role of the Maastricht Treaty on European Union. Of course the treaty would go further in creating a more highly-developed form of supranational European constitution, but key developments in relation to regulation can be found in earlier community developments independent of the Maastricht process. Second, this emerging constitutional structure has important implications for the nations of Central Europe described in this book. Czechoslovakia, Hungary and Poland are already linked to the Community by Association Agreements, and the new agreements all note that the final objective of these nations is Community membership. Though the precise structure of the obligations that will apply to them will, of course, be subject to negotiation, clearly Community membership will have important implications for their economic structures.

The existing elements of Community law that provide a structure relevant to privatization concern the boundary to be drawn between public and private sectors, the procedures to be adopted for privatization, and the style of regulation to be employed.

At first sight, the question of the boundary between public and private and the systems of property ownership to be adopted would not seem to be a subject for Community law. After all, Article 222 of the EC Treaty is explicitly neutral as regards public or private property ownership (see also *Costa v. ENEL* [1964] ECR 585). More relevant would perhaps seem to be the European Convention on Human Rights in relation to which the European Court of Human Rights has indicated that in principle *nationalization* could breach the right to peaceful enjoyment of possessions under the Convention where compensation was so small as not to be reasonably related to the value of the property taken and there was no legitimate public interest to justify this (*Lithgow v. United Kingdom* [1986] 8 EHRR 329). Nothing in the Convention, however, limits the scope of privatization in a way comparable to the provisions in certain national constitutions reserving tasks to the public sector. Nor does it require the private ownership of particular economic sectors, and the principles in the Convention have been adopted in Community law by the European Court of Justice (see *Hauer v. Land Rheinland-Pfalz*, case 44/79, [1979] ECR 3727).

Nevertheless, there are a number of ways in which Community law provides substantive constraints that are likely to have a profound effect in relation to privatization and may also shape the future divide between public and private enterprises. Thus in the area of public utilities one can see the beginnings of a community model of utility enterprise emerging as the result of the process of liberalization of telecommunications, energy, transport and postal markets. The general thrust of this is clear; the Commission is seeking to open up markets through the limitation of exclusive rights for public enterprises and by requiring the separation of regulatory functions from the operation of the service. It is also requiring increased transparency of relations between governments and utility enterprises and transparency in the conditions of access to regulated markets. At the same time, the concept of services of a general economic interest partially exempted from competition provisions of the Treaty by Article 90(2), is being progressively narrowed, a theme made explicit in the Commission's *Twentieth Report on Competition Policy* (Commission of the European Communities, 1991: 12) and also important in the development of the case law of the European Court of Justice (see, for example, on telecommunications *British Telecommunications: Italy v. Commission* [1985] 2 CMLR 368 and case 18/88 *Regie des Telegraphes et de Telephones v. Sa 'GB-INNO-BM'*, judgement of 13 December 1991). It would, of course, be wrong to see this as a sudden imposition of a clear philosophy of the role of a European utility; proposals have met formidable political obstacles and, particularly in the more recent examples, remain vague on key points. Nevertheless, despite the formal neutrality on privatization, the underlying orientation corresponds closely to the model chosen for the privatized utilities in Britain, in particular through the requirement of a separation of regulator and enterprise (see, for example, case 271/90 *Spain v. Commission*, case C-281/90 *Belgium v. Commission*, and case C-289/90 *Italy v. Commission*, judgement of 17 November 1992, CJEC). Indeed, the withdrawal of exclusive rights removes one central justification for public ownership.

A somewhat similar thrust can be seen in the currently highly controversial question of State aids to public enterprises. A directive was issued by the Commission in 1980 requiring the provision of information on public funds paid to public enterprises directly or indirectly and on the purposes to which the aids were put, and this was strengthened in 1985. As regards public investment, the current position of the Commission was summarized as follows in the *Fourteenth Report on Competition Policy* (Commission of the European Communities, 1985, point 198):

> The theme of the provision of equity capital according to standard company practice in a market economy is the guiding principle adopted by the Commission. If it can be shown clearly that the State is acting in the same manner as would a private person in the market sector of the economy, then the presumption is that there is no question of State aid. If, on the other hand, the State is acting because the commercial sector would not intervene in the case in question, then there is a presumption that State aid is being granted.

The test has also been confirmed by the European Court of Justice: '. . . the test is . . . in particular, whether in similar circumstances a private shareholder, having regard to the foreseeability of obtaining a return and leaving aside all social, regional-policy and sectoral considerations, would have subscribed that capital in question' (*Belgium v. Commission* [1988] 2 CMLR 331, para. 13).

Perhaps the most politically controversial example concerned the provision of capital by the French government to Renault. The conservative Chirac Government had attempted in 1987 to change the legal status of

Renault to bring it closer to that of a private company, and this was to have been accompanied by a writing-off of debts. The change in legal status did not prove possible to implement and was dropped after a change of government in 1988. This provoked an investigation by the Commission, which demanded repayment of the write-off on the grounds both of the failure to change the status of the Company and failure to keep to the terms of a restructuring plan (Commission of the European Communities, 1990, point 187). Events were overtaken by the conclusion of an agreement to exchange equity stakes between Renault and Volvo, for which a change of legal status was a prerequisite, and this was then swiftly implemented. After a further inquiry by the Commission a compromise was reached under which half of the amount involved in the write off was repaid; Renault is now a candidate for privatization after another change of government. The issue of close scrutiny of financial dealings between governments and public enterprises remains a live one, however, and will no doubt be of profound importance in the preparations for privatization in, for example, Italy.

Once more one finds an attitude of principle on the part of the Commission highly relevant to the question of the role of public and private enterprises within an economy. Put at its simplest, what is the point of nationalization if public enterprises have to be treated by the State exactly as private investors would treat a private enterprise? To quote a *Financial Times* leader, 'Once it becomes clear that State ownership of industry confers no special privileges its appeal, in France and elsewhere, will rapidly evaporate' (*Financial Times*, 19 March 1990). One should add also that of course the notion of the conditions for the legitimate provision of capital is by no means straightforward; there is no simple pattern of market behaviour that can be identified as that of the private investor, and in fact a great deal of discretionary assessment will be necessary on the part of the Commission (for an outline of the principles used see Commission of the European Communities, 1992). Nevertheless, the point is clear; whilst the measures to liberalize the markets of public utilities will have profound effects for this type of public enterprise, those on State aids will also have a profound effect on more market-oriented public enterprises.

Moreover, policy on State aids has also had a more direct effect on one aspect of the privatization process itself; that of valuation and pricing. In our discussion of the peculiarities of the British privatization process we saw that the British government had extensive freedom under domestic law; it could treat sales of public enterprises just as a private seller could, subject only to *ex post facto* scrutiny by the National Audit Office. Community law has now imposed *a priori* constraints on the pricing process even in Britain in the form of scrutiny of privatization arrangements by the Commission before they are implemented. For example, the sale by British Shipbuilders of its Govan subsidiary was subject to Commission approval; one of the issues examined was whether the price paid for shares in the subsidiary was unduly low as that would have amounted to a State aid. Again, the sale of BREL (the British Rail engineering subsidiary) was referred to the Commission after an objection from a rival company. The sale involved the writing off of £64 million of loans by BR and the Commission considered that this amounted to a State aid, though it was cleared subject to the requirement of annual reports from the government on the implementation of the company's restructuring plan. In a slightly different context, the Commission recently required repayment of an unlawful element of State aid arising from the sale of land to Toyota by an English local authority for a new factory at below its full commercial value.

The most famous recent example of such scrutiny is, the sale of the Rover Group to British Aerospace. The original plan for the sale of the car business envisaged BAe paying a price of £150 million whilst the government would have injected £800 million into the business to wipe out debts. However, before the deal was finalized the Commission required that the injection be reduced to £469 million plus £78 million regional assistance. The sale went ahead, ostensibly on this basis, but in the course of a Public Accounts Committee investigation of the deal a confidential memorandum from the Comptroller and Auditor-General was leaked to the press showing that the government had made secret concessions of £38 million to ease the sale and that these had not been notified to the Commission. Further sums emerged later and the Commission decided that British Aerospace should be required to repay £44.4 million immediately and perhaps a further £40 million in 1991. This was challenged in the European Court by British Aerospace, a challenge upheld on the ground that the Commission had chosen the wrong procedure for recovering the aid (case 249/90, *British Aerospace plc and Rover Group Holdings v. Commission*, judgement 4 February 1992). The Commission has now issued a new decision requiring repayment after using a different procedure. The Commission also hinted that in future it would be unsympathetic to closed bids as part of a privatization; in the Rover case, British Aerospace had been granted sole negotiating rights. The Commission now routinely examines the financial arrangements for privatizations in advance of implementation.

It is thus evident that Community law has become of profound importance both in fixing the role and extent of the public sector and in shaping the financial arrangements involved in privatization, and it would be possible to give other examples such as the role of the acquired rights directive on the terms and conditions of employees in the privatization process, and the procurement directives in opening up transparency in relations between governments and enterprises contracting with them. One can draw a similar conclusion through an examination of the effects of Community law on the regulatory systems that have played such an important role in this book. The

Commission has examined particular aspects of the regulatory arrangements adopted after privatization, for example in the case of electricity privatization in Britain. Thus it assessed the role of the 'fossil fuel levy' designed to provide a continuing subsidy to unprofitable nuclear generating capacity. Although it found the levy compatible with Community law, the period for which it was to run was reduced from fifteen to eight years.

More important than these individual interventions is, however, the fact that in a number of areas, for example in environmental regulation, we are seeing an incipient conflict of regulatory styles. As suggested earlier, much post-privatization regulation in Britain remains dominated by governmental powers unstructured by any system of rule-making and with minimal procedural protections. Bargaining is central to such regulatory systems, and means of legal redress are virtually non-existent. Indeed, these characteristics represent a well-established style of British regulatory practice (Vogel, 1986). In other nations self-regulation has been seen as a promising means of avoiding the problems of regulation by formal legal norms, and the ambiguities concerning the role of law in former Communist countries have posed serious problems as to the effectiveness of such formal norms. By contrast, regulation originating at the Community level can be characterized by a greater reliance on legal devices and specifications of standards, and opens up much greater possibilities of legal challenge to governmental decision-making (Macrory, 1990, and on the inadequacy of implementation of directives by informal means *Commission v. Belgium* [1982] 2 CMLR 622). This may lead to a more litigious system of regulation, and may also lead to the specification of more precise procedural protections for those affected in the process (c.f. *Union Nationale des Entraineurs v. Heylens* [1989] 1 CMLR 401), something seen also in the area of procurement, for example through the requirement of a remedy in national law against certain abuses of the contracting process. Ironically, the growing role of the European Communities may lead to a style of regulation more closely resembling that of the United States.

## CONCLUSION

Politics matters in shaping the privatization process, and even more so in shaping the environment after privatization. Even a relatively neo-liberal government such as that of Mrs Thatcher in Britain was not prepared to leave privatized enterprises simply to the play of market forces, and a number of political devices were adopted for influencing their behaviour. Moreover, regulation is far from the Weberian ideal of rule-based administration; it is highly pragmatic and discretionary. Even the British RPI − X pricing formula, the closest technique available to pure rule-governed regulation, has turned out in practice to involve highly discretionary judgements. Regulation thus raises crucial questions of institutional design and accountability.

The stress on the importance of national characteristics in this work suggests that it would be unhelpful to attempt direct emulation of British experience, especially in Eastern and Central Europe where attempts to apply simple plans relying on it could do immense harm. However, any discussion of national styles needs to take into account the fact that decision-making is now largely on a European-wide basis through the role of the institutions of the European Community, and this is replacing central elements of national style, especially in the regulatory field.

This raises two related problems. The first is so familiar as hardly to need repeating; the Community institutions themselves suffer from a serious 'democratic deficit' so that accountability for *their* decisions is seriously lacking. In this sense the emergent supranational constitution, whilst relatively sophisticated in some methods of legal accountability, lacks a basis of democratic legitimacy, and at the time of writing nothing in the Maastricht process seems likely to change this. The second, related problem, is that of the implicit political worldview contained in the emergent supranational constitution. All constitutions contain such a worldview, what Frazer has described as a norm 'that seeks to impose a certain form of economic organization concomitant to the social, political and cultural choices that constitute European society' (Frazer, 1990), though the pre-Federal nature of the European Community and the need to gain consensus from national governments has meant that the view implicit in the Community Constitution has been little debated and often left ambiguous. Once more the Maastricht process should have provided an opportunity for the debate of the choices involved but, at least as seen from within Britain, such debate has been conspicuous by its absence.

The discussion so far has tended to emphasize the role of the emerging supranational constitution, not just as creating greater transparency but as favouring a model of enterprises close to that adopted by the Thatcher Governments in Britain. However, the political model inherent in the Treaties is not exclusively dominated by such an approach; as Frazer has put it:

> even a brief consideration of other Community economic policies will reveal that the competitive system is only one Community method, and not a template for the creation of an economic system . . . The acceptance of a deeply intrusive regulatory regime for the agricultural sector prevents the free market transaction being characterised as a Community constitutional norm.
>
> (1990: 615 and see 620–3)

What is needed is more analysis of the fundamental political and economic assumptions that are implicit in the contribution of the emerging Community constitution to economic life. Thus what form of constitutional principle and theory can best justify the peculiar combination of markets and rights emerging in the Community? What constitutional rights are presupposed by market transactions and what rights prevail over market outcomes? Which of the elements of national uniqueness we have identified are worthy of preservation? The fact that there are strong incentives for the avoidance of such basic questions at the political level does not mean that they are inappropriate for constitutional analysis.

## BIBLIOGRAPHY

Commission of the European Communities (1985) *Fourteenth Report on Competition Policy*. Brussels.

Commission of the European Communities (1990) *Nineteenth Report on Competition Policy*. Brussels.

Commission of the European Communities (1991) *Twentieth Report on Competition Policy*. Brussels.

Commission of the European Communities (1992) Practice Note: re State Aids to Public Undertakings, 64 CMLR 399.

Frazer, T. (1990) Competition policy after 1992: the next step, *Modern Law Review*, 53, 609.

Macrory, R. (1990) The privatization and regulation of the water industry, *Modern Law Review*, 53, 78.

Vogel, D. (1986) *National Styles of Regulation*. London, Cornell University Press.

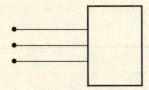

# INDEX

SHEFFIELD HALLAM UNIVERSITY LIBRARY
CITY CAMPUS POND STREET
SHEFFIELD S1 1WB